Best wishes

Living with the Enemy

Dorchester's Great War Prison Camp

The happy lot of the captive Hun: scenes at Dorchester prison camp.

Living with the Enemy
Dorchester's Great War Prison Camp

Brian Bates

Step-Up Books

Published by Roving Press Ltd under their Step-Up Books Imprint
4 Southover Cottages, Frampton, Dorset, DT2 9NQ, UK
Tel: +44 (0)1300 321531, www.rovingpress.co.uk

Distributed by Brian Bates, 15 Garfield Avenue, Dorchester, Dorset DT1 2EY, tel. +44 (0)1305 263824.

First published 2016 by Roving Press Ltd

ISBN: 978-1-906651-299

British Library Cataloguing in Publication Data
A catalogue record for this book is available from the British Library

Front cover photos: *'Receiving the newspapers' and orderlies preparing for Christmas 1914 (courtesy of the Keep Military Museum).*
Back cover photos: *Inside one of the three wooden huts used as hospital wards. Eating soup (courtesy of the Keep Military Museum). The happy lot of the captive Hun.*

Set in 11.5/13 pt Minion by Beamreach Printing (www.beamreachuk.co.uk)
Printed and bound by Beamreach Printing (www.beamreachuk.co.uk).

Contents

Preface

When I began the research for this book I was amazed that so few local people knew of the existence of Dorchester's POW camp. So much so that when I began giving lectures on the topic I called them 'Dorchester's best kept secret'. Perhaps, on reflection, it is not so surprising that such an event should have disappeared into the mists of history. After all, little remains of the old artillery barracks which housed the camp and it is now covered by the Grove Industrial Estate, and those walking their dogs on Poundbury hill fort[1] have no inkling that they might be treading on the former football pitch or making their way through the guards' camp.

The wooden huts that accommodated the prisoners were eventually cleared from the site, but two of them remain in the area. One can be found in Northernhay, used by local auctioneers Jeffs, whilst another was moved to Winterborne Monkton, a hamlet just south of the town, and has been used as a residence ever since. The present owner informed me that when electricians had occasion to enter into the roof space they found some German names carved into a beam.

Despite the absence of physical evidence of the camp's existence, a few people continue to remember those who spent a part of their lives as captives in Dorchester. The Town Council has taken on the job of maintaining the memorial in St George's Cemetery, and each year on Remembrance Sunday a short service is held there, when prayers are said and wreaths laid on the very spot where the bodies of the dead once lay.

In 2014, as part of the WW1 commemorations, the camp came to the attention of a wider audience when the BBC made a short radio broadcast and television programme about it.

It is hoped that this book will help keep the candle of remembrance burning.

Two of the surviving prisoners' huts from the Poundbury POW camp.

1 Poundbury hill fort began life as a Bronze Age enclosure. It is roughly rectangular in shape and its ramparts command views over the River Frome and Dorchester town.

Foreword

One hundred years on, it is clear that the First World War affected every community and, indeed, every family. Much of this has been well covered by the political, military and social histories of the period, but Brian Bates in this volume covers new and largely unexplored ground. Following many years of original research, he presents a detailed and fascinating picture of life for German prisoners of war between 1914 and 1919 in the British POW camp at Poundbury, Dorchester.

This book is a welcome addition to our local historical knowledge. In a town of 9000 inhabitants, to have a camp of up to 4500 prisoners was a huge addition. As Mayor of Dorchester, I confess to a sense of pride that even amidst the heightened passions of war, a prisoner could describe the townspeople's attitude as 'exemplary'.

The author also throws an interesting sidelight on our literary history. Thomas Hardy was a frequent visitor to the Poundbury Camp and he welcomed prisoners to work in his garden at Max Gate. He observed the similarity between the local Dorset dialect and the German language. English and Germans, he commented, were 'Kin folk, kin tongued'. His sympathies were with the sufferings of innocent victims of war, of whatever nation.

Finally, this book illustrates aspects of our national history. Poundbury was the headquarters for a whole network of POW camps across southern England, so this detailed local study is likely to be representative of a much wider national picture. It is also interesting to note that at the very time that the allied leaders were disastrously planning extremely punitive reparations against the Germans, the Poundbury Camp Commandant and the people of Dorchester were planning full military funeral honours for the unfortunate German victims of the 1918 flu epidemic and, quite exceptionally in any British town, the erection in Fordington Cemetery of a German War Memorial.

These seeds of humanity and tolerance have since borne much fruit. Each year on Remembrance Day, the Mayor, Councillors and citizens of Dorchester conduct a simple act of remembrance at the German War Memorial, and for over 40 years, Dorchester has been officially twinned with the German town of Lübbecke. I feel immensely privileged to be President of the Dorchester–Lübbecke Society and that, for me, Lübbecke is my second home.

Peter Mann paying his respects at Dorchester's German war memorial in Fordington Cemetery.

I am delighted to contribute this foreword and to commend Brian Bates' work, I hope, to a wide readership.

Peter Mann

Peter Mann moved to Dorchester, with his wife Sheila, from Hertfordshire in 1983, when he took up the post of Chief Inspector of Schools with Dorset County Council. But his connection with the Dorset education system goes back further than that, when he was a pupil at Broadstone First School in Poole. After his family moved to Devon he went to Tavistock Grammar School, before studying modern history at Merton College, Oxford, where he attended lectures by eminent historian A.J.P. Taylor. Peter has a long connection with Dorchester United Church and an equally long association with Dorchester's twinning society with Germany, and has been its President for the last 12 years. He has served on Dorchester Town Council and became Mayor in 2014.

Acknowledgements

I would like to take this opportunity to record my appreciation of the many people who contributed towards the production of this book. My wife Beth has shown immeasurable patience and understanding, and, when I was struggling with the text, always managed to pluck from the air the precise word I was trying to find. My knowledge of the German language is limited and I must thank Gabi Dorst, Maria Jacobson, Penelope Lane, Anna and Stephen McLuckie and Eduard Schneider, all of whom helped with translations of the German sources.

Many people, some relatives of guards, have been very generous by providing photographs and personal stories; their names are noted in the book against each image. Thanks are also due to the International Red Cross, the Keep Military Museum, the Mill Street Housing Society, the Dorset History Centre and the Dorset County Museum for allowing me to use images from their archives. Photographs not accredited are from my own collection. I would also like to thank Sid Brown and Derek Pride for allowing me to photograph items from the camp. Peter Mann kindly agreed to write the Foreword. Last but not least, thank you Julie and Tim Musk, of Roving Press, for providing advice and seeing the book through the editorial and production processes, with their usual thoroughness and professionalism.

Profits from this book are being donated to
the work of the Refuge Welfare Committee.

Abbreviations

Bde	Brigade
Btn	Battalion
Capt.	Captain
Col	Colonel
DWAC	Dorset War Agricultural Committee
Gen.	General
ICRC	International Committee of the Red Cross
Lt	Lieutenant
Maj.	Major
NCO	Non-Commissioned Officer
POW	prisoner of war
Pte	Private
RAMC	Royal Army Medical Corps
RDC	Royal Defence Corps
Rgt	Regiment
Sgt	Sergeant

A note on sources

Primary sources on Dorchester's POW camp are scarce. They mainly consist of reports made by individuals or teams of officials from neutral countries who visited the camp throughout the War, and can be seen in the respective national archives. Other than the odd reminiscence, like that of Gunther Plüschow, they provide the only first-hand written accounts of what life was like in the camp.

However, there are some contemporary photographs and a remarkable short film depicting daily life. Many of the photographs in this book, particularly those taken inside the camp, come from a book published in 1916 by the British authorities, at the request of the American Ambassador in Berlin, and were due to be shown at a War Exhibition in Württemberg, Germany. The images in the original book, which were taken by members of the Photographic Unit of the Royal Flying Corps, cover six of the largest camps in Britain – Donnington Hall, Alexandra Palace, Dorchester, Handforth, Lofthouse Park and Eastcote – and were, to quote the Foreword of the book, taken to indicate 'That the excellence of the conditions under which the prisoners live are in striking contrast to the regime which obtains in many of the prisoners' camps in Germany', adding, 'It is only necessary to recall the horrors of Wittenberg

This illustration comes from a volume, published in 1919, of the photographs taken of the Dorchester camp. The drawing shows the plight of the POW. The shackle of a locked padlock pierces a bleeding heart, alluding to the anguish of the prisoner, and retains an anchor, a symbol of hope, and a cross depicting spirituality. The key to freedom is peace, indicated by the word PAX, the name of the Roman goddess of peace. The wording below the illustration translates as 'Pictures from the POW camp Dorchester. What annoys us in life you can enjoy in pictures.' (Courtesy of the Keep Military Museum.)

and Gardelegen[2], to appreciate the admirable organisation of the prisoners' camps in Great Britain.'

Such statements raise the question of whether or not the photographs taken were merely for propaganda purposes, and to some extent they were. But the real question is how accurate and reliable a picture do they give of what life was really like in the camps? The book assures the reader that 'It should be understood that the prisoners were left entirely free to choose whether they would be photographed or not. The photographers had very explicit instructions that no prisoner was to be photographed without his consent and that neither compulsion nor persuasion was to be employed to induce anyone to form part of a group. These instructions were carried out and it is an indication of the readiness of the prisoners to allow themselves to be photographed that repeated requests were received by the authorities that copies of the photographs should be placed on sale at the camps.' Despite its obviously intended purpose, the photographs do give a good indication of certain aspects of camp life.

The 12-minute film of the camp is quite remarkable. The quality of it is excellent and there is none of the jerkiness one associates with early cinematography. The Imperial War Museum catalogues it as a British propaganda film, made in 1917, and it certainly sets out to make a point. The second caption of the film reads, 'These pictures illustrate how the thousands of German prisoners captured by the British are treated in captivity.' Another caption reads somewhat like a holiday brochure: 'THE CAMP AT DORCHESTER – One of many such camps – is beautifully situated within a few miles of the sea.' It then goes on to show many aspects of life in the camp. We see the men at roll call and queueing up to receive their pay. There are scenes of the prisoners at play, on the sports field, in the reading room and with their pet rabbits. Other parts show prisoners busy in the carpentry workshop, the camp bakery and the timber store. In many of the scenes it is very obvious that the men know that they are being filmed. Aside from the men, the film gives a good indication of how the camp was laid out.

To call either the photographs taken in 1917 or the film 'propaganda' is, in my view, a little harsh. The word implies that the information given is either dishonest or exaggerated and, in the case of the Dorchester camp, I do not believe that it was. Yes, certainly the authorities wanted to show the rest of the world how good we were at looking after our prisoners, compared to the Germans, but there was another, more important motivation, which

2 Serious cases of typhus broke out in both of these camps, due to insanitary conditions.

explains, perhaps, why the photographs were going to be shown in Germany. One of the ominous shadows which was always present during the War was that of reprisals, and by showing the Germans how well their men were being looked after there was the hope that they would reciprocate.

The German national archive, the Bundesarchiv, has very little information on the camp, but it does house a copy of the one surviving edition of the camp newspaper, the *Deutsche Blätter des Kriegsgefangenenlagers Dorchester*[3], and a collection of theatre and concert programmes for performances given by the camp theatre club and orchestra. The newspaper tells us little about the feelings of the men, but it does give some useful information on the camp's social and sporting life.

Much of the information in the book has come from newspapers, particularly local ones, which present their own problems as a source of information. In a time of war they can be prone to patriotic exaggeration and sometimes they get the detail wrong. As to their accuracy, in many cases local reports, like the funeral of a prisoner or the arrival of a new batch of internees, were made by representatives of the press who were there at the time and offer first-hand experiences. The articles that appear in the foreign newspapers, mostly American, are based on either the official reports of delegations who visited the camp or those made by press representatives. Some of the information appears to be based on hearsay or what someone was purported to have overheard. Nevertheless, providing one keeps this in mind, they do offer another perspective and should not be dismissed.

3 Translates as 'German leaves of Dorchester prisoners of war camp'.

A group of civilian and military prisoners marching through the village of Charminster, a village 2 miles north of Dorchester, in March 1915. This image was made into a postcard, for sale to the prisoners. (Source: A.J. Brown.)

Dorchester on the Eve of War

On the eve of the Great War a visitor to Dorchester, the county town of Dorset, would have found a thriving, confident community, aware of its rich historic past. The town's population had increased significantly during the previous 30 years, resulting in a surge in house building in all quarters and, as a consequence, local businesses were thriving.

The cornerstone of the town's economy was agriculture, particularly the raising of sheep. In the 16th and 17th centuries Dorchester had been a prosperous wool and cloth town, exporting to France and Flanders, yet, when the cloth trade waned and finally disappeared, sheep farming did not. In October 1886, 20,000 sheep were penned on Poundbury, waiting to be sold. In Dorchester, the job of serving the farmer remained. Lott and Warne's foundry, at the bottom of Fordington High Street, made ploughs, harrows and water pumps, whilst the Eddison and Matteo Steam Plough Works made engines and road rollers, and hired out steam ploughs.

The population of Dorchester was estimated to be around 9,500 in 1911, and there were all kinds of businesses there to support it. Ernest Parsons ran his grocery shop in High East Street, Thomas Benjafield his bakery in Monmouth Road and Robert Membury his ironworks in Colliton Street, all of whom lost sons in the War. Mr Channon, who was still making horse-drawn carriages at his works in High East Street, had now turned his skills to building a new craze, the motor car. His young sons, who were equally as mechanically minded, built a biplane based on the Wright brothers' design, and flew it from the nearby ancient hill fort of Maiden Castle.

Dorchester's status as a county town did not just depend on its importance as a market centre. It was also the place where the offices of most of the county-wide judicial and administrative services could be found. Dorchester had been granted the right to hold Assizes by Henry VIII and with that came the running of the county gaol. Also, organisations like the Board of Guardians, the County Council and the county health services had their headquarters in the town.

It was an age of civic pride, which, in Dorchester, became tangible when the Borough Gardens were built in 1896 and later embellished with a fine clock tower and large fountain, provided by local worthies. The two railway stations welcomed tourists, curious to see the town portrayed in *The Mayor of Casterbridge*, penned by the author Thomas Hardy, who lived at Max Gate, within walking distance of the town centre.

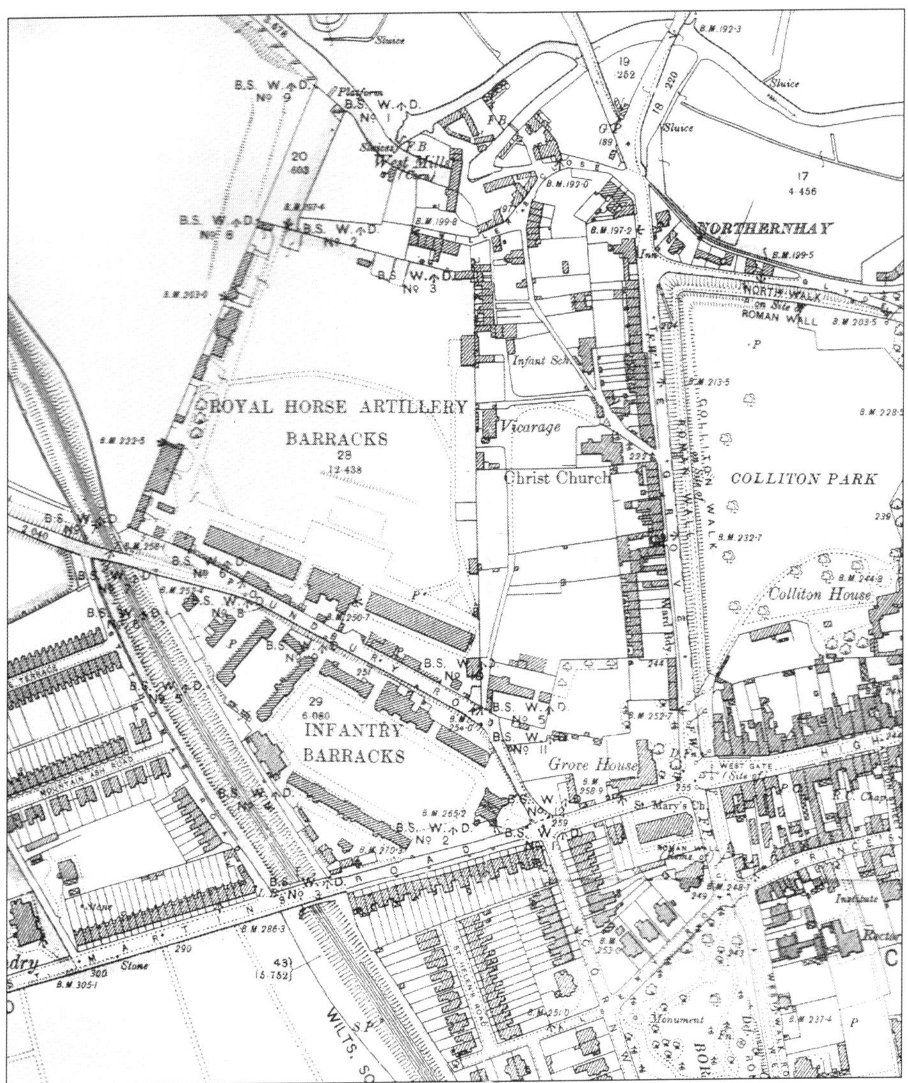

This map of 1901 shows just how close the Infantry Barracks and the Royal Horse Artillery Barracks were to adjacent residential properties and the town. (Source: M. Russell.)

Dorchester had another reason to be proud. It was the home of the county regiment, the Dorsets, which was housed in the Depot Barracks situated on the western outskirts of the town and was a significant presence. Soldiers used the local shops and public houses, occasionally appearing before the local magistrates when they over-imbibed, and married local girls. Some military personnel decided to settle in the town after retirement. One such military man was Col John Tweedie, but he was not an officer of the county regiment. John had been a colonel in the Royal Horse Artillery, which had its own barracks next to that of the Dorsetshire Rgt. During the War this barracks took on a very different role, when it became the centre of attraction as a place of incarceration for prisoners of war.

When war came, the town was transformed overnight, the local newspaper, the *Dorset County Chronicle and Somersetshire Gazette* describing how it was like 'a leagured town in the bustle, excitement and the many and varied uniforms seen in the throng, hurrying to and fro'.[4] During those early days, troops from a variety of regiments arrived on foot and by train, but it was not long before a very different style of uniform was seen marching through the town. Those who wore it were the enemy and instead of being greeted with waves and cheers they were received with silence and suspicion. The people of Dorchester were about to spend 5 years living with the enemy.

4 *Chronicle*, 15/8/1914.

The National and International Context

The First World War was truly a 'Great War'. The number of countries involved, the number of military personnel fighting each other and, of course, the number of casualties were without precedent. Another aspect of the War which was without precedent, but one that is largely forgotten, is the considerable number of prisoners of war that were imprisoned by the belligerent nations. The last time Britain was required to entertain military prisoners in any great numbers was during the Napoleonic Wars (1803–1815), when over 100,000 were held.

Whilst there was little precedent for the welfare of prisoners, there was a set of agreed rules about how warfare should be conducted, set out in the Hague Convention of 1907. One section is devoted to the welfare of prisoners of war and contains the basic principle that they should be treated humanely and not as criminals. Importantly, it also puts the duty of care on governments, by saying that those captured are the responsibility of the country concerned and not the individuals who seized them. The details of the convention cover areas regarding accommodation, food, work and pay. (The articles of the convention relating to prisoners of war are set out in Appendix 1.)

In August 1914, the British government had neither the administrative apparatus nor the means to accommodate the impending influx of detainees. The same was true of the German government, and many of the claims made by both sides in the early part of the War, about the mistreatment of prisoners, was a result of this chaos rather than any overt wish to harm them.

The administrative system that emerged for the welfare of prisoners operated at different levels. Internationally, a number of organisations were involved. Charities worked with governments and visited the camps, whilst the Red Cross played a major role by keeping records, providing information and acting as an intermediary in cases of repatriation.

Neutral countries also played an important part. At the beginning of the War, the USA, a neutral country at that time, was asked to monitor the treatment of prisoners. This included visiting POW camps set up by both the Entente and the Central powers.[5] The USA operated through its embassies,

5 The Entente powers consisted of Britain and its allies; the Central powers consisted of Germany and its allies.

for example in London and Berlin, and sent teams of diplomats, sometimes accompanied by newspaper reporters, into the camps. Typically, in the British camps they not only observed and spoke to the camp authorities but also had the opportunity to speak to the prisoners themselves, unimpeded, and their reports with any recommendations for improvement went to the countries concerned. These inspections were reported widely by the press, which seemed eager to tell the public of what life was like behind the barbed wire. So much so that some foreign newspapers arranged for their own correspondents to visit the camps. See Appendix 2.

At the national level, the government department that concerned itself mostly with the running of the camps was the War Office, which oversaw the building of the camps and provided the personnel to run them. The Home Office took an interest in civilian internees and their camps. One essential organisation that came into being at the start of the War was the Prisoners of War Information Bureau, which found its origins in the Hague Convention. At its headquarters at 49 Wellington Street, Strand, London, the staff spent much of their time answering relatives' questions about their imprisoned loved ones. Much of this information came from the register it compiled of all alien enemies, combatant and civilian, who were interned in any part of the British Empire. As the number of prisoners grew, so did its staff, which had increased to 300 by 1918 and were answering up to 400 enquiries each day from Germany alone.

Locally, several agencies became involved with the prisoner system. Local authorities, such as county councils, applied to use detainees in projects like road building and, when a scheme of work for prison labour on farms was finally established, it was to the county agricultural committees that the War Office looked to organise things on the ground. The camps themselves were run by commandants from the military, but they relied a great deal on self-governance by the prisoners.[6]

It is difficult to say how many camps operated throughout the War, because some, like the one at Blandford, came and went, but one estimate suggests that there were about 600 operating in 1918 and 1919.[7] Camps were designated according to function and to social considerations. Initially, some camps, including Dorchester, held both civilians and military personnel, but by 1915 the majority of civilians had been moved to their own camps, the largest of which was Knockaloe on the Isle of Man, which held a total of about 30,000 prisoners. Camps were also divided on class lines. Holyport in Berkshire

6 See page 12.
7 Panayi.

and Donnington Hall in Leicestershire were both manor houses and became homes for officers, whilst Other Ranks found themselves in all kinds of accommodation. In London, the Alexandra Palace was requisitioned, as was Cunningham's holiday camp on the Isle of Man. Others were accommodated in a disused engineering works, some in a disused distillery, and others were even put into a skating rink. Work camps appeared wherever they were required. The largest was built at Slough in Buckinghamshire, as a depot and repair facility for mechanical transport; the smallest were single farms scattered around the country.

It was within the rules laid down by the Hague Convention, and the administrative bureaucracy which grew of the initial chaos, that Dorchester, one of the largest of the camps, operated from the beginning of the War until well afterwards.

A Camp Is Born

When the British government finally realised at the start of the War that they had made little preparation for the housing of prisoners of war in Britain, the War Office sent immediately a telegram to local military commands telling them to make temporary arrangements, at once, to accommodate and feed prisoners of war. Buildings could be requisitioned and camps put in place, but not near defended ports. The areas were to be wired to keep prisoners in. Authorities were also told to report on what longer term permanent arrangements were to be made in their area. Prisoners would be arriving through the ports of Sheerness, Dover, Portsmouth, Plymouth, Southampton, Queenstown[8] in Ireland, and Rosyth. For the Dorset military authorities there was one facility in their area that admirably fitted the bill.

Dorchester's Royal Horse Artillery Barracks, built between April 1794 and July 1795, was situated in the north-west sector of the town, just a few minutes' walk from the town centre. The site is now covered with industrial units and forms the Grove Trading Estate. Few of the original buildings remain and those that do are distinguished easily by their russet-red brick, so typical of much military architecture. One such building, located in Poundbury Road, is now home to Dorchester's Territorial Army, C Company 6th Btn the Rifles, but in its previous life it formed one of two long barrack blocks which had stabling on the ground floor, with stalls for 28 officers' horses and 160 troopers' horses. Above these there was accommodation for 4 Quartermasters, 12 Sergeants and 164 Privates. Between the two blocks was another, smaller building, where there were 21 rooms for officers and their servants. Opposite these buildings, lining the road, were the straw barn, two cookhouses and the guard room.

Walking further down Poundbury Road from the direction of the town, a right turn at the next corner leads onto the industrial estate, where the eye is met immediately by a low-level building with three large arched windows. It is now used as business premises, but behind it, attached to the wall, there are clues to its former use. These are metal tethering rings, for this was the indoor riding school, used to train many a mounted soldier. Further down the hill can be found another structure of red brick, this time with a porch, which until recently was in a poor state of repair but has been restored most sympathetically. This building was the camp hospital, with its wards,

8 Queenstown is now called Cobh.

The building with the arched windows is the former artillery riding school, used as a carpentry workshop by prisoners.

operating theatre and dental surgery. Other camp buildings included the engine house, barns, stores, blacksmiths shops, canteen and kitchen.

For nearly 150 years the rattle of harness and the clip-clop of hooves could be heard throughout the town, as cavalry and artillery units came and went. Ironically, on one occasion the camp hosted a group of German Hussars who acted as a guard of honour to King George III, and on another it was inspected by Field Marshall Blücher, our great ally at the Battle of Waterloo. In 1914, however, the artillery barracks was empty.

The choice of Dorchester's artillery barracks as a POW camp had certain advantages. First, it had many of the facilities for the accommodation of large numbers of men, although, at the time, the authorities could have had no idea that 1 month into the War it would be full to overflowing. Second, because the camp was located on the edge of the town, when the need for expansion arose there was plenty of room to spread out in the direction of Poundbury hill fort.

Together with Horsham and Olympia, Dorchester was the first of the British Great War POW camps to be established. Some of the first batches of prisoners were housed in the rooms above the stables and the officers' apartments, each room containing two to four bunks, whilst others occupied sundry buildings around the camp. It was not long before all the buildings were full and bell tents had to be erected on the recreation ground to deal with the overflow. However, this was far from satisfactory, particularly with the impending winter coming along. With over 1,000 prisoners in the camp by the end of August 1914, and an indeterminate number of additions to come, clearly, a more permanent solution was needed. It was therefore decided to construct a hutted camp, and building began in December, within the confines of the barracks. Each hut was clad in weatherboard,

By the end of August 1914 the camp already had over 1,000 prisoners. When the artillery barrack accommodation was full, bell tents were erected on the recreation ground.

measured 50×16 ft and housed between 30 and 40 men. The floors of the huts were raised above the ground, resting on pillars, heating was provided by iron plate stoves and each hut was supplied with electric light. All of the prisoner accommodation within the artillery barracks became designated as Compound 1.[9]

This photograph shows the road that led up to the recreation ground. On the right in the distance are the first of the huts that were built to extend the camp. The building in the right middle is the camp hospital. Each hut has chimneys for the stoves that were installed, and the electricity connections can be seen, as can the fire buckets hung on the walls. Today, this whole area forms part of the Grove Industrial Estate. (Courtesy of the Keep Military Museum.)

9 Some sources refer to the camp having two compounds, whilst others refer to Camp 1 and Camp 2. For the sake of clarity I have used the word Camp for the whole establishment, and the word Compound for its two parts.

As more and more prisoners arrived in the camp it was obvious that a further extension was required, and the first phase of this took place between the boundary of the artillery barracks and the Great Western Railway Weymouth to Bristol line. When Mr Lowry of the American Embassy visited on 1 December 1915, he noted that the 3,447 men present were housed in 113 huts, each housing 30 men, and there were plans to increase the size of the camp further.[10] At first, it was intended that the additional accommodation

These photographs (courtesy of Dorset County Museum), which show the major part of the camp, were taken after it was evacuated in November 1919. The above photograph was taken from Poundbury Road Railway Bridge and shows the first extension, outside the boundary of the artillery barracks. Outside the picture, to the right, were more huts and the barrack buildings. The long white fence, which does not look particularly secure, probably separated Compound 1 from Compound 2. The building with the arched roof (centre) was the timber store which was replenished by trains pulling into the siding.

The photograph below shows part of Compound 2. There were more huts to the left of the picture, together with three hospital wards. The lamp, shown bottom centre, may have been part of the latest technology system installed at the beginning of the War.

10 *Charleston Sunday News*, 2/1/1916.

would be built by the prisoners, but the Dorchester trade unionists objected to this and insisted that local labour was used, although later on prisoners were used to build huts and undertake other construction work in the camp. The new huts were erected on the other side of the railway line and spread toward Poundbury hill fort. This new part of the camp was designated as Compound 2.

For security, the high wall surrounding the artillery camp was fitted with angled metal stanchions, made by the local firm of Thurmans, to which were attached lines of barbed wire. Outside the walls, platforms were built on which were placed sentry huts. Surrounding the rest of the camp and the recreation field were three lines of metal fence posts supporting horizontal lines of barbed wire. There were no watch towers.

The fact that the railway bisected the camp was of great benefit. From one of the tracks, two sidings were built into the camp, to bring in items such as the huge quantity of timber required to build the huts. It does not appear that they were used for the arrival of prisoners.

Unfortunately, we know little of how the camp operated. The first Commandant was a Col Block, but little mention is made of him and it has not been possible to identify him. He was succeeded by the 60-year-old Col Henry O'Brien Owen, who had retired from the Royal Field Artillery in 1905. Owen oversaw the growth of the camp, until the end of 1915 when he resigned. His resignation may have been because of his age, but another influencing factor may have been the spate of escapes from the camp. The man who took over from Owen was Lt Col Henry Charles Bulkeley, another retired army officer, almost as old as Owen, at 57, who had served with the 4 Btn West Yorkshire Rgt. Bulkeley appears to have remained in charge up until it closed. Each had an Assistant Commandant; a Capt. Mitchell was acting in this capacity under Col Owen, but in 1919 a Capt. A. Le Gallais, 1 Btn Royal Scots Fusiliers, was in the post. Le Gallais was a serving soldier who could not have been at the Dorchester camp for very long, because he was taken prisoner

Lt Col Henry Bulkeley, Camp Commandant from 1916. (Source: www.Europeana1914-1918.eu (Traugott Pfledere).)

in Flanders on 30 October 1914 and was not repatriated until 9 December 1918.

It appears that, other than the guards, the camp operated with very few British military personnel. One report says that, except for a few commissioned officers assisted by four sergeants and a small squad of Red Cross officers, there was not a single British soldier inside the compound,[11] whilst another, published around the same time, tells its readers that it took a staff of 3 officers and 7 NCOs to run the camp.[12] When it came to the day-to-day affairs it seems that there was a remarkable level of self-governance, the prisoners looking after their comrades. It is likely that, as in other British camps, each hut had an elected a representative who reported to a prisoner NCO. He, in turn, was responsible to a camp leader, who liaised with the British Camp Commandant. In the spring of 1919, Offizierstellvertreter Otto Schoenekes of the 360 Infantry Rgt was the camp leader of Compound 1, and Offizierstellvertreter Max Milotta of the 10 Infantry Rgt was the leader for Compound 2.

Gunther Plüschow,[14] when writing about his stay in Dorchester at the beginning of 1915, hinted at the important role played by the camp leaders. Speaking of one of them, probably the leader of Compound 1, he said, 'Special praise is due to the Senior German prisoner, a Warrant Officer from Munich. He was a merchant and spoke English fluently. A most remarkable personality. He was really the soul and veritable guardian angel of the camp. Nothing was done without his approval and directions. He was the English Camp Commandant's right-hand man, and without him

Drawing by Kurt Polent entitled Schreibstube[13] Vom Lager 2 (Office of Compound 2). (Courtesy of the Keep Military Museum.)

11 Report on visit to the camp by neutral powers in January 1916, reported in the *Reading Eagle*, 23 January 1916.

12 *Calgary Herald*, 19/2/1916.

13 The word *Stube* can refer to a barrack room or a study. In this instance the word *Schreibstube* may be an office or a classroom.

14 See page 35.

I do not know what would have become of the English, who did not possess the slightest vestige of talent for organisation. It was simply extraordinary how this Warrant Officer looked after our people and acted as go-between with the English. The English officers knew full well what a help to them he was.'[15]

Despite Plüschow's view of the administration, he had a great respect for the British officers running the camp, commenting that, 'Captain Mitchell and Major Owen especially deserved praise for the treatment of our men. Both were true regulars, had been through many campaigns and battles, and knew how to handle troops. These two and the English Medical Officer[16] presented the men with games, gymnastics, outfits and a band, and did whatever they could for them.'[17]

Similar plaudits were given to Bulkeley when the American Dr Taylor visited in September 1916. 'Commandant Bulkeley, who had seen many years of East Indian service and is fully familiar with the physical care of men, takes an active and personal interest in everything that pertains to the subsistence of the prisoners of war under his charge.'[18]

The *Reading Eagle* was equally as complementary, commenting that, 'The camp seems to be fortunate in the personnel of its directing officers. Major Bulkeley[19] is a typical prison warden. He is a humane man with a decided sense of humour and his personal attitude towards his charges makes a ready response. He is a regular army officer who has seen much service and knows when to be firm, but he stated to the correspondent that he seldom has occasion to exercise his duties of discipline. The prisoners are almost automatic in their observance of military etiquette.'

There were, of course, instances where individual prisoners had to be disciplined, and these are illustrated elsewhere in the book, but there is no contemporary evidence of any mass disobedience or rioting. However, something did come to light in 1976, when in a letter to the *Dorset Echo*, Thomas Carter, a 14-year-old electrician working in the camp in 1915, claimed that he was locked in with 2,000 Germans who had mutinied over poor rations. He was verbally abused but not harmed in any way.[20] Thomas was not the only civilian to work in the camp. In the Government film, British

15 Plüschow.
16 Maj. W.B. Cosens.
17 Plüschow.
18 Taylor, September 1916.
19 Other sources refer to Maj. Bulkeley. He was promoted to temporary Lt Col on 16 December 1915.
20 *Dorset Echo*, 26/8/1976.

men in suits and cloth caps and plans in their hands are in the carpenters' shop and another is present when the prisoners are receiving their pay.

Taking care of the prisoners within the camp's confines was only part of the job for the camp authorities. Dorchester was chosen as the parent camp for the Southern Command Area, which comprised the counties of Dorset, Devon, Cornwall, Somerset, Wiltshire, Hampshire, Warwickshire, Worcestershire, Gloucestershire, Oxfordshire, Buckinghamshire, Berkshire and part of Surrey. It was reported in August 1917 that Dorchester was managing 6,246 prisoners in work camps, employed as fruit pickers, miners, carpenters, masons, machinists and in many other jobs, over this wide area.[21]

The administration of the Dorchester camp should not be underestimated. In terms of population, it was, at the time, larger than the Dorset town of Wareham, and all its residents had to be fed and accommodated and their physical and spiritual needs cared for. There were the added complications of having residents who were confined to a small area, were not free to come and go as they pleased and were living in cramped conditions with people they did not necessarily want to have a bed next to. The success of the camp is best described by two of the delegations from neutral powers who made inspections. Naville and Van Bercham concluded, after their visit to Dorchester, that it was the best organised camp they had visited, while de Sturler after his visit reported that 'Dorchester camp well deserves its reputation as a model camp which is well established and kept in good working order' (see Appendix 2).

21 *Milwaukee Journal*, 7/8/1917.

The Early Weeks

The people of Dorchester could not have failed to notice the frantic work going on at the empty artillery barracks in order to convert it into a POW camp. The erection of lines of barbed wire fencing, elevated sentry post huts and floodlighting indicated that it was not just a case of preparing it for its usual use of housing British soldiers and their horses. The period between the beginning of the War and the arrival of the first batch of prisoners was less than a week and the local press had no time to report on the preparations, if, indeed, the purpose for which the site was to be used was known generally. It was not until after the first prisoners arrived that the *Chronicle* hinted of the town's interest, when it reported that 'The greatest public interest has been revealed in the preparations for their reception, and the people have eyed with curiosity the many elevated sentry boxes and beats, and the double row of unclimbable barbed fencing by which their exercise ground is enclosed.'[22] One wonders what conversations took place and what rumours circulated the town during that first week of the War. Dorchester was a safe town and there had been no cause for alarm since fears of Napoleon Bonaparte landing at Weymouth, 100 years earlier. Now, Durnovarians were entering again a period of uncertainty, made worse by the prospect of having the enemy living in their midst. Whatever their fears, the townsfolk did not stay indoors, hiding behind their curtains. Instead, they came out in their hundreds to view the new residents.

On 9 August, several companies of the 3rd Battalion Scots Fusiliers had moved into the new camp to await the arrival of its first guests. They did not have to wait long. The very next day, news went about the town that a batch of prisoners were due to arrive on the 1.50 train at Dorchester West railway station. Before the train's due time of arrival the station yard and the platform were cleared of all except those who had business there, and the Town Council took the precaution of closing Poundbury Road, between the council depot and the camp.

The 18 prisoners that stepped from the train were not, perhaps, what the crowd expected, because, as the *Chronicle* put it, 'There was nothing at all martial or bellicose in their appearance. They were all neatly dressed and several were chubby boys. One of the leading Germans was stolidly puffing

22 *Chronicle*, 27/8/1914.

on his pipe in bravado.'[23] Accompanied by a detachment of the Fusiliers, these men, who had been brought from Plymouth, were marched down Cornwall Road, the children in the crowd cheering the escorting Scotsmen and the adults eyeing the prisoners in silence. If the townsfolk were expecting to see foreign soldiers, sailors and airmen striding towards the barracks then they were disappointed, for all the early prisoners brought to the camp were to be civilian internees.

That afternoon it became known that a further group of prisoners were to arrive on the 6 o'clock evening train, this time at Dorchester South station, and again groups of townsfolk assembled in the area and along the roads to the Royal Horse Artillery Barracks. This much larger group of 89 were also dressed in civilian clothes, and it was now the turn of the *Western Gazette* to be free with its language, describing them as 'a motley collection, a good number of whom were shabbily dressed and decidedly "down at heel"', whilst others of them were 'well dressed, of gentlemanly appearance and who appeared well-to-do', adding that the latter were doubtlessly spies who had been arrested in the previous few days.[24]

Well-dressed civilian prisoners being escorted from Dorchester South Railway Station by policemen and armed soldiers. (Courtesy of Dorset County Museum.)

That evening, half the town appears to have congregated outside the camp in Poundbury Road, so much so that the road had to be closed again and the crowd dispersed. Another attraction, other than the camp's new residents, which may have brought great numbers out was to see the floodlighting system that had been installed. It was the latest technology in lighting and had only been invented that year, consisting of 15 lamps of 2,000 candle power, which gave twice the luminosity of anything yet produced. It had

23 Ibid.
24 *Western Gazette*, 14/8/1914.

been installed by Messrs Brooking & Company, under the supervision of the Dorset Electricity Supply Company.

The imprisonment of civilian internees in Dorchester was the result of the government's position on civilians of enemy countries living here in Britain. It was determined in the first week of the War, when Parliament passed a bill which restricted the rights of aliens, who were now required to register locally and were prohibited from entering restricted areas like ports, dockyards and military installations. Neither were they allowed German language newspapers. Travelling around was severely restricted and could not be done without a pass. One woman who contravened this rule was Marie Sophie Holzer, who lived in Ferndown, in the east of the county. Marie appeared before the local court for travelling more than 5 miles from her registered place of residence, namely her place of work, without first obtaining a permit. She was fined £5. One internee at Dorchester used the law to his own advantage. Adolf Carl Knop, who was born a German but became a British subject in 1906, was arrested on 5 September 1914 at his home in Southampton and held in Dorchester until 17 November. Knop sued Col Block, the Camp Commandant, for wrongful arrest and false imprisonment and won his case, which was settled out of court by the payment of compensation.[25]

For those aliens living in restricted areas the new laws were particularly harsh and could lead to tragic results. Frank Borgmann, who was aged 51, had being living in England for about 40 years and resided at 1 Park Terrace, Lennox Street, Weymouth, with his wife Pauline. Both of them had worked in the town, he on the cross-Channel boat service and she as a nurse, but they had both lost their jobs because of the War. Consequently, the couple found themselves in financial difficulty and they had been summoned for the non-payment of rates. Their plight was made worse when they received an order under the new laws, telling them that they had to leave the area by noon, on 31 July 1914. On the morning of the due date a bailiff turned up at the house to demand furniture in payment for the rates and, in desperation, Frank went to the local police station to tell them that he could find nowhere to go. He was reported to have said, 'Take me to prison, put me into a camp, or shoot me.'[26] What happened next was described at an inquest by Mrs Borgmann, who was not an enemy alien. She said that her husband had pleaded with the Chief Constable, but he said that he could do nothing as it was not his decision. Accordingly, she and her husband returned home, with Frank in a

25 *London Times*, 15/6/1917.
26 *Western Gazette*, 6/11/1914.

very depressed state. Later, Pauline saw her husband drinking from a bottle in the scullery. The bottle, which she took away from him, contained spirits of salts,[27] bought for cleaning brass. The doctor was called but there was no hope for the man, who had a very painful death. The jury found that Frank Borgmann had committed suicide, while of unsound mind.

A somewhat more bizarre case relating to the new regulations was heard by the Dorchester Borough Police Court in November 1914. A man, who gave his name as Robert Hammond, was charged with being an alien enemy in the prohibited area of Dorchester without a permit. The prisoner had been observed in the neighbourhood of The Grove, very near the Depot Barracks, and caused some commotion, claiming, when challenged, that he was a German spy. As a result he was taken into custody and when questioned claimed that his mother and father were living in Germany. He stated that he, however, was born in South Africa and that he wanted to go and join General De Wet's army.[28] He added that 'Germans are every bit as good as Englishmen' and that England was not going to be 'top-dog' much longer. Evidently Hammond showed no indication of being German, he had no accent, and when he was put before the magistrates he claimed to be deaf. The play being performed before the court took a distinctly comical turn as questions and statements were put to the prisoner in very loud voices. When the Chairman of the Bench, who happened to be Alderman Allen, Dorchester's Mayor, asked the man what he had to say for himself, he changed his tune and said that he was not an alien after all, claiming that the whole thing was a joke, helped on by an excess of alcohol. Then, his previous convictions were read out, one of which showed that the defendant, whose real name appeared to be Robert Smith, had stolen an overcoat from the said Robert Hammond, together with his name. The magistrates accepted that he was not a German, but his ill-timed humour cost him dearly, when he was sentenced to 3 months imprisonment with hard labour.[29]

In addition to the restrictions imposed on all enemy aliens, certain males were to be interned. These included those thought to be spies or dangerous and, significantly, males between the ages of 17 and 42 who could not prove that they were exempt from military service. On 7 September 1914 it was decided that all enemy reservists should be interned, priority being given

27 Hydrochloric acid.

28 Gen. Christian De Wet was a Boer War general who fought for independence from British rule. He and other Boar War Afrikaner leaders protested against South Africa's support of the British Empire and attempted a revolt against the British government.

29 *Western Gazette*, 13/11/1914.

to the unmarried and the destitute. As one can imagine, these internments caused much emotional and financial distress, as families lost their loved ones, many of whom were the sole wage earner. Some of the internees had resided in Britain for many years and had well-established businesses, whilst some British businesses, like hotels and restaurants in London, relied heavily on German and Austrian waiters. The plight of these, mainly innocent, victims was recognised by the Government, and the War Office was considering releasing some of the internees, but any thought of this was nipped in the bud by public outrage following the sinking of the British passenger liner *RMS Lusitania*, which resulted in riots in Liverpool, which spread across the country.

By December 1915 the total number of persons interned in the UK was 32,272[30], and during the early months of the War, Dorchester received a steady flow of them. One early group of about 70, who were Devon residents of enlistment age, were rounded up and held in Sidwell School, Exeter, before being sent on to Dorchester, and a group of 100 reservists arrived on 10 December, followed by another on the 12th.[31]

Some of the unluckiest of the prisoners were merchant seamen, who either found themselves in the wrong port at the wrong time or were crews of captured merchant ships. One such group of 93 seamen arrived in the town on 17 August and further batches continued to arrive before the month was out. The *Western Gazette* reported that on the 24th a group of 381 'Austrians' arrived at the camp, after being landed at Falmouth.[32] At the same time, another party arrived from Falmouth, passengers who had been taken off the Dutch steamship *SS Potsdam*, which had been captured by the British cruiser *SS Diana* on its way between New York and Germany. Mainly consisting of Germans, with a few Austrians and Hungarians, the prisoners included the musician Carl Hermann and Bruno Schmidt-Reder, who later wrote about his experiences in the camp.[33] Four of the men, who were thought to be German diplomatic staff, were set free and repatriated 3 months after their capture.

It was not long after their arrival that the new additions to Dorchester's population were becoming the talk of the town, causing the author Thomas

30 Jackson.

31 *The Midland Daily Telegraph*, 13/8/1914.

32 *Western Gazette*, 28/8/1914. The number of Austrians given by the newspaper is very close to the number 381, mainly Germans that came off the *SS Potsdam*. It is possible that the *Gazette*'s reference to Austrians was incorrect.

33 See page 42.

Hardy to comment in a letter to his friend Edward Clodd,[34] 'There are 1,000 prisoners of whom we get glimpses through the chinks. The prisoners, they have already mastered enough broken English to say, "Shoot Kaiser", and oblige us by playing "Good Save the King" on their concertinas and fiddles. Whether it is meant sarcastic I cannot tell.'[35] To his friend Edmund Gosse he wrote, a few days later, 'We have more than 1000 prisoners here, Germans and Austrian, and they have to be kept apart, the latter fighting with the former and charging them with having made the trouble.'[36] To the Rev E.C. Leslie he wrote, 'Dorchester is more or less full of soldiers and German prisoners.'[37]

In addition to national differences, the bringing together of men from different walks of life and classes was bound to be a challenge. The *Chronicle* described the prisoners as 'very mixed samples of Teutonic folk, embracing rough seafaring men, waiters, shop assistants, and labourers, and also officers and gentlemen of position and substance, who can afford to do something

Men from all branches of the service and social classes lived cheek by jowl. Here the prisoners are mustering on the parade square of Compound 1. The camp notice boards can be seen, where news and events were posted. (Courtesy of the Keep Military Museum.)

34 Source of letter: Florence Hardy. Edward Clodd, English banker, writer and anthropologist, who had many literary and scientific friends, including Thomas Hardy.

35 Letter dated 28/8/1914.

36 Letter dated 10/9/1914.

37 Letter dated 25/12/1914.

to minister to their needier fellow countrymen all being, by the chances of war, companions in "misfortune" – if indeed it be a misfortune to be secure from the perils and privations of war, and to be comfortably housed and fed in idleness.'[38]

Any fears that the local population may have had were likely lessened by a couple of early incidents. The *Aberdeen Journal* in August 1914 reported that one of the German reservists arrived at Dorchester armed with a banjo, and as the procession of guards and captives moved off to the Artillery Barracks he played the tune 'Annie Laurie', much to the amusement of the escorting Scottish Fusiliers. Similarly, the *Chronicle* reported on another batch of prisoners who arrived at Dorchester South Station on Sunday 16 August, pointing out that, 'Several of the men brought musical instruments with them, which enabled quite a creditable wind and string band to be formed, so that the prisoners can now solace themselves with instrumental as well as vocal music. On Sunday afternoon and evening, when the public of Dorchester flocked up to Poundbury curious to catch a glimpse of the captives, quite a concert was given within the wire enclosure. The sonorous air of the Austrian National Anthem was recognised towards the close; and, apparently in grateful recognition of the considerable and generous hospitality with which these hostages are being treated, the selections closed with the English National Anthem.'[39] This may well have been the performance witnessed by a local woman who wrote to her friend the following month, saying that she had attended a concert given by the prisoners at the Barracks.

The War brought with it a heightened sense of security. For example, one prominent local man who experienced the new exigencies of war was, with towel over his arm, making his way to Dorchester's swimming pool. When passing over Poundbury Railway Bridge, next to the prison camp, he was arrested by a guard and promptly marched off to the guard house, where he remained for several hours until he could verify his identity.[40] Another man was arrested for signalling, allegedly, from Poundbury hill fort to the prisoners in the camp, but an application for a court martial was dismissed by the General commanding the Southern Military District and the case came to nothing. The *Western Gazette*, reporting on the case, said, 'It appears that there was nothing to show that he was anything but

38 *Chronicle*, 20/8/1914.
39 Ibid.
40 Ibid.

a loyal and patriotic British subject'.[41] Intrigue from inside the camp came when it was reported that one of the sentries had shot a homing pigeon from one of the roofs which had a letter written in German concealed under its wing.[42]

Escape from the camp was, of course, always possible and it must have been an anxiety for many townsfolk, particularly in the early months, and later, when news started to come through about alleged atrocities done by German soldiers to civilians in France and Belgium[43] It was not long before the first rumour of an escape swept through the town. Just after 10 pm on a Monday night, a shot was heard coming from the direction of the camp. The next day a rumour circulated that a prisoner, who had been shot in the leg by sentry whilst trying to escape, was lying in the military hospital. The truth of the matter proved to be somewhat less dramatic. It turned out that one of the prison guards, a Scots Fusilier, unused to the rifle which he had been issued with, accidently discharged a round into the air. When reporting on the incident the *Chronicle* concluded its report by saying, 'It is by such things that rumour is fed'.[44] The warning had little effect on Durnovarians because just a few days later another rumour was being passed around the town that another prisoner had escaped. This time two shots rang out from the direction of the camp, just after midnight. It was another false alarm, this time caused by the newly installed, state-of-the art floodlighting system, which had fused, plunging the camp into darkness. In the event of such an occurrence the sentries at either end of the camp were ordered to discharge a round to bring out the guard.

Because Durnovarians had lived cheek by jowl with the military for so long they were, perhaps, a little more relaxed about the requirements of the wartime situation, to the extent that the *Chronicle* felt obliged to publish the following notice: 'As it is a novel experience for us to be living under war conditions in Dorchester, and as many persons do not seem disposed to take it seriously, but regard the posting of sentries and their challenges as a curiosity not altogether devoid of amusement, it may not be superfluous to warn our readers that the military precautions are "no joke" and that, if they are in the neighbourhood of either of the Barracks they cannot be too

41 *Western Gazette*, 18/9/1914.

42 *Western Gazette*, 25/9/1914.

43 Several alleged atrocities done by the enemy appeared in the press, encouraged by the British government, for propaganda purposes. Accusations included the raping and mutilation of women, cutting off the hands of young men, gouging out the eyes of civilians and bayoneting babies.

44 *Chronicle*, 27/8/1914.

careful to respond promptly to sentries if challenged, and not indulge in ill-timed levity.'[45]

Nor was the novelty of the camp confined to the locals, because it evidently became something of a tourist attraction. For example, one woman living in Bournemouth wrote, in a letter to a friend, that she might stop off in Dorchester on her way home to have a peep at the camp, adding that, 'J – is rather curious to get a glimpse of the German prisoners, as he was not with us when we saw them last week.'[46]

---

45 Ibid.
46 *Western Times*, 18/6/1916.

Comings and Goings

The camp population was by no means static, and what started as one-way traffic became two-way when the camp underwent a major change in use. Eventually, it would be exclusively for military prisoners. The process began in October 1914 when a contingent of 200 military arrived, mostly sailors, on a special train from Edinburgh.[47] December was particularly busy, as 450 civilians left for the internment camps on the Isle of Man and 600 departed for Handforth POW camp in Cheshire. Meanwhile, a further 500 military prisoners arrived from the camp at Frith Hill in Surrey on 15 December. One group of 350 who left at this time were part of an exchange agreed between the German and British governments. They were men who were either over or under the age of enlistment.

Prisoners going about their every-day business. (Courtesy of the ICRC.)

Evidence that the class system was alive and well in 1914 was seen when 300 officers and men of better classes were transferred to the prison ship *SS Canada*. The *Canada* was one of nine prison ships used to hold civilian and military prisoners, which were moored off the Isle of Wight and in Portsmouth Harbour. Although modern, the ships were not popular with the prisoners. The limited space on board heightened the feeling of confinement, which was exacerbated by the fact that the well-off could pay for better and roomier on-board accommodation. From the British point of view, there were also reservations. Some Members of Parliament suggested that the ships could be put to better purpose and that the cost of chartering them, £86,000 per month, was excessive, one MP suggesting

47 *Western Gazette*, 5/11/1914.

that it would be cheaper to take the whole of Grosvenor Square and furnish it handsomely for the prisoners. Concerns were also expressed about the security risk of having three of the ships anchored in Portsmouth Harbour, with the possibility of prisoners obtaining sensitive information and passing it on. Thus, by the summer of 1915, all of the vessels were returned to their traditional tasks.

On 18 December 1914 the press reported that the camp at Dorchester was practically empty, but at the very time of writing military prisoners were on their way.[48] During the same week, a batch of 200 arrived from the Aldershot military barracks, escorted by members of the Hampshire National Reserve, consisting of civilians, soldiers, sailors and submarine crews. Another consignment of 500 also came from Aldershot and the reporter present at their arrival at Dorchester South station observed that 'The prisoners were a medley lot of several line regiments, wearing the bluish-grey uniform of which we have heard so much, relieved with inconspicuous red facings and piping, and in some cases blue shoulder straps. Among the infantry were a sprinkling of cavalrymen in top boots, some of them spurred. They were mostly heavy-built and stocky. Many were carrying baggage and belongings, and many tons came by train.' The writer was especially impressed by how the men formed up into columns of four after getting off the train, putting it down to the military discipline of the Germans.

When Mr Jackson of the American Embassy visited the camp on 4 February 1915, he noted that the camp was exclusively combatant, holding 909 soldiers and 25 sailors plus a group of 25 German boys brought from a reformatory school in Belgium, although a photo on a postcard, taken in March 1915, shows clearly civilian prisoners among a group on an exercise march through the village of Charminster.[49] Another change in policy would see the disappearance of the officer prisoners from Dorchester, turning it into a camp for NCOs and Other Ranks. Men like Otto Köehn and Gunther Plüschow were transferred to places like Donnington Hall in Leicestershire, Dyffryn Aled in Denbighshire and Holyport in Berkshire, taking with them their German servants, of course. These movements did not go unnoticed by some members of the press and public, who claimed that they were going to places where they would lead a life of relative luxury.[50]

48 *Western Gazette*, 18/12/1914.
49 See photograph facing page 1.
50 *Reading Eagle, 23/01/1916.*

Submariners captured from German U-boats were a particularly controversial class of prisoner. The *Chronicle* told its readers that part of the crews of three German submarines, the *U8*, the *U12* and the *U14*, were also making their way to the county town.[51] This simple event was the last act of a drama that had been taking place between the respective governments of Germany and Britain. It began in February 1915 when Germany announced unrestricted submarine warfare on commercial shipping in waters around Great Britain, warning that the safety of crews of British and neutral ships could not be guaranteed. This enraged not only a large proportion of the public at home but also the First Lord of the Admiralty, Winston Churchill, who decreed that from then on all captured submarine crews would be placed in naval prisons as criminals, instead of being sent to a detention camp. Such reprisals were not prohibited by the Hague Convention, but some voices claimed that it was wrong to treat submariners differently as they were only acting under orders. The very valid point was also made that such reprisals might lead to similar actions against British prisoners, which was precisely what happened.

Despite the reservations, as the number of British unarmed merchant ships sunk increased, so did public outrage. On 4 March 1915 the German submarine *U8* was sunk in the English Channel and 29 members of crew were saved. The Admiralty declared that, 'The officers and men taken prisoners from German ships have received the treatment appropriate to their rank and such courtesies as the service allows. The Board of admiralty do not, however, feel justified in extending honourable treatment to the 29 officers and men rescued from the submarine *U8*. This vessel has been operating in the Straits of Dover during the last few weeks and there is strong probability that she has been guilty of attacking and sinking unarmed merchantmen – Persons against whom such charges are pending must be the subject of special restriction, cannot be accorded the distinctions of their rank, or be allowed to mingle with other prisoners of war.'[52]

As a result of this policy the crew of the *U8* were sent to the Royal Navy Detention Barracks at Chatham, instead of a POW camp. Others were more outspoken in their view. Mr Frederick Harrison of Bath wrote a letter to the *London Times*, in which he said that the crew of the *U8* were not prisoners of war but common pirates and murderers and suggested that they should be tried at the Old Bailey.[53] Another correspondent, Mr Holt,

51 *Chronicle*, 17/6/1915.

52 *London Times*, 9/3/1915.

53 *London Times*, 10/3/1915.

offered a prize of £500 to the captain of the first merchant ship to sink a German submarine.[54]

When the *U12* was sunk in the North Sea on 12 March and the crew were incarcerated in Devonport Barracks, the ensuing publicity was picked up by the German government, which, in reprisal, picked out 39 British officer prisoners for segregation. The next act of the drama came on 5 June when the *U14* was rammed off Peterhead in Aberdeenshire, resulting in the capture of 27 prisoners. At the same time the British Government declared a change of policy towards submariners, ending their segregation. The catalyst for this change in policy may have been the replacement of Churchill as First Lord of the Admiralty or simply that it was a futile gesture. A more cynical view, perhaps, was that it had something to do with the fact that the British prisoners chosen for segregation were all titled or members of prominent families.

Throughout 1915 the camp at Dorchester continued to increase in size, to meet the increasing numbers of prisoners of war. In October a large contingent of 1,000 prisoners arrived from Southampton, on route for Dorchester, all captured during the Battle of Neuve Chapelle,[55] and when a member of the Associated Press was shown around the camp by Maj. Bulkeley in December 1915, he noted that all areas of Germany were represented and many units of the German army. He also observed that as far as possible these units were kept together and that there was hardly a hut that did not contain an English-speaking occupant. Two of the prisoners, who did not look to be more than 16 years old, told the correspondent that they were taken with their submarines, somewhere in the North Sea.

Not all the prisoners during 1915 were incoming. When Otto Koehn, for instance, made his escape he took advantage of the fact that a group of older prisoners were being repatriated,[56] and the *Western Gazette* reported of an occasion when three men were part of a prisoner exchange.[57] It told its readers that one of the Germans involved was 'a notability reputed to be very wealthy, and certainly since he has been under detention there have been conspicuous evidences of affluence', adding that, 'To a certain extent there were many regrets, mingled with the congratulations at the departure, for the reason that the particular prisoner in question had been very liberal to

---

54 Ibid.

55 The Battle of Neuve Chapelle was fought between 10 and 13 March 1915 in the Artois region of north-west France. During this battle, 1,200 Germans were taken prisoner.

56 See page 104.

57 *Western Gazette*, 20/11/1914.

his fortunate brethren around him'. The newspaper went on to say that this particular guest of the War Department was to be exchanged for a General who had been in Germany at the outbreak of the War, and that when the prisoner left the compound to catch a train to London the camp band turned out and gave him a musical send-off. The German concerned must have been of considerable standing to be exchanged for a General. The other two prisoners involved followed a day or so later. The three men were most likely civilians, as the British and German governments did not agree on the exchange of military personnel until later in the War, and even then they had to be severely wounded or seriously ill. In most cases it was easy to recognise if a Dorchester prisoner was wounded severely, but it was not so easy to decide if a man was seriously ill. Consequently, any prisoner diagnosed as suffering from tuberculosis or mental illness was not eligible for repatriation, because it was thought that once he returned home he might recover and once again be fit to fight.

Doubtless, those Germans who returned home were delighted, but this was not always the case. On 20 December 1915 the *Scottish Evening Telegraph and Post* ran the following headline: 'Germans Refuse to Leave Dorchester'. This referred to a report that some members of the German Red Cross, who were not prisoners but had probably been working in the camp, had refused to leave the camp and had to be compelled to return home. The *Telegraph* had no doubt that the reason for their reticence was because the camp was so comfortable.

A group of prisoners, some of whom were captured during the Battle of the Somme, in 1916 pose for a photograph. (Courtesy of the Keep Military Museum.)

A change in government policy resulted in 1,400 prisoners leaving Dorchester in the spring of 1916, not to their homeland but back to the battlefield. At this time, supplying the British Army on the Western Front with everything required to continue the War was a major undertaking, resulting in congestion at the bases at Le Havre and Rouen. Not enough troops could be spared from the fighting to clear the backlog, so the French Government was asked to supply men to unload ships bringing in materials and munitions, to work felling trees and to quarry stone. The French response was that they could not spare any of their men, so another solution had to be found. That solution was to establish POW companies to do these jobs. In addition, and more controversially, POW companies were to work behind the lines on labouring tasks.

At first, the idea was opposed by the British Commander in Chief, General Haig, on the grounds of expense, the practical difficulties of housing and feeding a large number of prisoners in the war zone, and the danger of escapes. However, he was persuaded to try it. Perhaps foremost in his mind when he decided to do so may have been the realisation that every soldier who was capable of fighting would be required for the big push in the area of the Somme, planned for the summer. Haig was not the only person to have reservations about the use of POW companies. Lord Newton[58] feared, correctly as it turned out, reprisals, with British prisoners being sent to hazardous places or having to endure poor treatment. The Hague Convention stipulated that prisoners were not permitted to carry out work related directly to the conduct of the War, but, in this instance, the British Cabinet determined that the tasks involved did not contravene this rule. The German reaction to the British scheme was to complain that German prisoners were being held behind the lines, working and living in poor conditions, with inadequate food. Visits by American inspectors showed that this was not the case, but the German Government was not convinced and, in retaliation, moved 2,000 British prisoners from camps in Germany to Poland, with the threat that their conditions could alter for the worse. These prisoners remained in Poland until the spring of 1917, when the German prisoners were returned to Britain.

The men bound for France in April 1916 were not the only departures from the camp that year. In July, 581 wounded prisoners were repatriated to Switzerland.[59] When the first Swiss legation visited the camp on 29 and 30 March 1917 (following the USA joining the War), the report it produced showed comparative population figures of 3,409 on 1 January 1916, 3,543 on 1 January 1917 and 1,575 when they visited in March. They noted that the accommodation consisted of three barrack blocks and 112 huts, each

58 Thomas Wodehouse Legh, 2nd Baron Newton PC, DL (18 March 1857–21 March 1942), was a British diplomat and Conservative Member of Parliament. In 1916 he became Assistant Under-Secretary of State for Foreign Affairs and was put in charge of two departments at the Foreign Office, one dealing with foreign propaganda and the other with prisoners of war. In October 1916 he was appointed Controller of the newly established Prisoner of War Department, and in this position he negotiated the release of thousands of British prisoners of war.

59 Mark.

with 20 prisoners.[60] This drastic reduction of population occurred because 2,355 prisoners were listed as being employed in ten work camps, including Sandhill Park in Somerset and Bramley in Hampshire. The camp numbers peaked in April 1919, when there were 4,407 incarcerated, including 49 Austrians, 152 from the German navy and two German airmen.[61]

When peace came in November 1918, the main topic of conversation and rumour among the prisoners must have been 'when are we going home?' Unfortunately the answer would be some time in coming. The Armistice may have been signed, but as victors the allies dictated the peace, and no prisoners were going to be returned until the terms of the peace had been agreed, which did not happen until 29 June 1919, when the Versailles Treaty was signed. Dorchester's prisoners of war did eventually leave, the last ones on 20 November 1919, but there were few Durnovarians around to see them off. Their departure was very low key and warranted just a short paragraph

German prisoners enjoy a last meal before their journey home. (Courtesy of the Keep Military Museum.)

60 Ibid.
61 Ibid.

The prisoners make their way to Dorchester West railway station. The building on the right, now demolished, was the Great Western Hotel. (Courtesy of the Keep Military Museum.)

in the *Chronicle*: 'All the German prisoners of war, numbering several thousands, which were quartered at Poundbury, have been repatriated and the great internment camp will know them no more. To the majority of individuals their departure was practically unknown until it became an accomplished fact, because the prisoners left in large batches at night. The plateau at Poundbury, which has been enclosed by barbed wire, is once again open to the public and "young Dorchester" has not been slow in taking advantage of this old time privilege.'[62] The *Western Gazette* ran a similar article but added, 'During the horrors of war many thousands of them passed through the internment camp, while many remained in the compound for protracted periods, and the man is not known who would ever wish them back.'[63]

Homeward bound.

62 *Chronicle*, 20/11/1919.
63 *Western Gazette*, 21/11/1919.

The Enemy in Our Midst

As the early weeks of the War turned into months, Dorchester people got used to their new foreign inhabitants. By the end of 1914, prisoners were working on the streets of the town and in the local park, and some were employed in local businesses and households. For some, the relationship between town and prisoner became too familiar. In September 1914 a denial appeared in the local newspapers against accusations that had appeared in *The Globe*, a London evening newspaper. The accuser, who signed himself 'Middle Templar', claimed that some of the German and Austrian officer prisoners were being allowed to roam free about the town on parole and that they were spending freely in the shops. Moreover, he added that the prisoners were provided with their own free (captured) Viennese band, and, lastly, he felt that the nearness of the camp to Weymouth and the Naval Base at Portland was an unacceptable security risk.

The response to these criticisms came from Dr William Burrough Cosens, medical officer of the camp and a prominent local man. Taking Templar's points in turn, he wrote, 'In reply to the letter signed "Middle Templar", I am sorry he listens to gossip and then publishes it. We are not "monstrous" fools in Dorchester and can take care of Weymouth and Portland better than Middle Temple-Lane EC.[64] (1) We have 1000 prisoners of war in Dorchester camp. (2) No prisoner is allowed out on parole. (3) Prisoners have a band of their own, which they are wise enough to use. (4) "Officers" may be "spending a lot of money in the town". I hope they are but they are not allowed out to do so. "Middle Templar's" "facts" are fiction. I "confirm" this fiction, but deny the "facts" given him on "excellent authority".'[65] Cosens may have felt that he had put the accuser in his place, but that was not quite the end of the matter. The following week another letter was sent to the local newspaper, by a Mr H.A. Batchelor, saying, 'There is not so much "fiction" in "Middle Templar's" letter as is conveyed by Dr Cosen's letter. … I have seen three lots of prisoners out. I cannot say if they were officers or not; but they were certainly prisoners.'[66] Cosens nor any of the other camp representatives replied to this last pronouncement and the episode seems to have ended there.

---

64 Cosens assumes that Middle Templar is a member of the Inner Temple, one of the four Inns of Court, located in Middle Temple Lane, London, EC.

65 *Western Gazette*, 18/9/1914.

66 *Western Gazette*, 25/9/1914. The men that Batchelor spotted were probably going to a place of work or on an exercise march.

In a town where the young male population was being depleted day by day, the arrival of others, be they the enemy and unobtainable, aroused more than a passing interest to the local girls. The situation became too much for one anonymous correspondent, who felt compelled to write to the *Chronicle* suggesting that, 'The feather-brained daughters of Eve who congregate about the Dorchester barracks when the German prisoners are out for their daily walk should remember that they are English women!'

There are few recorded incidents that indicate how the general populace felt about the prisoners of war, but the little evidence we do have seems to suggest that they were treated generally with a mixture of sympathy and toleration, and occasionally overt kindness. Some, of course, perhaps for very personal reasons, simply saw them as 'the Hun, and the enemy'. There was one occasion when contempt and kindness showed their faces in one afternoon. George Squibb[67] was one of the guards escorting a group of prisoners on an exercise march on a summer's day. The procession made its way due south along the road to Weymouth and after about 4 miles reached the village of Bincombe. Since leaving Dorchester it had been an uphill slog all the way and, as it was a hot day, the prisoners complained that they were thirsty. Luckily, the group was very near to George's home, so he took them to his house, where his wife brought out jugs of water to the prisoners. Her act of kindness was not appreciated by her neighbours, who admonished her. In answer, she reminded them that every prisoner was someone's son, just like their own.

Prisoners singing on an exercise march. It was on one of these that George Squibb, pictured here middle right, with a moustache and carrying a rifle, took the prisoners to his house for refreshment. Prisoner Gunther Plüschow commented how the men loved to sing patriotic German songs. (Source: R. Hoadley.)

67 See page 127.

Acts of kindness came from both sides. Mrs Whitty remembers her mother telling her that, as a child, she and her sister were always sent to where the Germans were selling firewood, rather than the usual local outlet, because they always got more for their money and the Germans were kind to them. Other children, in the village of Winterborne St Martin, had fond memories too of the prisoners who worked on local farms. As the working parties passed through the village on their way back to Dorchester, the men threw peg dolls, which they had made during their break, to children who lined the roads.[68]

Other incidents that occurred in the workplace showed another side of human nature. One day in August 1919, a large group of prisoners formed a square on the parade ground in the camp. Inside the square were camp officials, a representative of the War Office, and Pte Bruckmann, who was there to be honoured for saving the life of a British pilot. A few weeks earlier, Bruckmann had been working with a group of other prisoners near Salisbury when, nearby, an aircraft crashed to the ground and burst into flames. At great risk to himself, the German private ran to the plane and pulled the pilot from the wreckage, saving his life. For his bravery the soldier was presented with a gold watch and a gift of money. A greater gift to him was that he was told that he would be sent home immediately.

Pte Bruckmann was not the only prisoner to be called away from his work to perform a brave deed. When a 15-year-old boy fell through the ice on a pond at Lytchett in Dorset,[69] a German sailor named Dellman, who had been working at a nearby brickworks, pulled him from the water, which was 15 ft deep. Dellman had had an eventful war. He was one of the survivors from the *SMS Blucher*, which was sunk at the Battle of Dogger Bank with the loss of nearly 1,000 lives, and, after being rescued and sent to Dorchester, he escaped and was recaptured in Weymouth.[70]

Although responsibility for discipline in the camp lay with the War Office, it appears that the prisoners were liable under English law if they committed a misdemeanour. One such case was that of Washen Synlvozenski, a Hungarian, who was not alone when he stood before the Borough Police Court on 21 September 1914. Also present was a contingent of the camp guard, three interpreters, one Rumanian, one German and one Hungarian, plus his accuser Hans Frommholz. The young defendant was charged with

68 Hearing.

69 The Lytchett referred to is probably Lytchett Minster, which had the Upton Brick Works in the vicinity.

70 *Taunton Courier*, 26/2/1919.

stealing a pair of boots from the latter. In giving evidence the plaintiff stated that he had taken the boots off to wash his feet and found that they had vanished when he went to put them on again. Five days later he spotted them in a trunk belonging to the prisoner. Through interpreters, Synlvozenski, who sobbed occasionally, said that he had found the boots, which he did not think were of any value. Col Block, the Camp Commandant, said that the defendant appeared to be a 'half-witted sort of a wretch,' who had recently found a sovereign and gave it up to his barrack leader. This act of honesty and the fact that he had already been held in detention for 10 days may have led to the court's decision to discharge him.[71]

Another case, which arose after the War ended, involved a boy who at the age of just 14 must have been one of the youngest prisoners to have been confined in the camp. The court was told, through Mr Herbert Richards, the official camp interpreter, that Heinrich Boraheurs was accused of stealing various sums of money belonging to other German prisoners. The lad had been under the care of a Capt. Fiscking, who explained that Boraheurs was due to be repatriated to Germany the next day with a group of Austrians and Germans. He informed the court further that he was anxious about the welfare of the boy and that if the Bench was prepared to release him he would look out for him. In the circumstances, the magistrates decided to sentence the prisoner to 1 day's imprisonment, which meant that at the rising of the court he was to be returned to the prison camp and leave the next day.[72]

Apart from the incidents where prisoners came into the public eye, either through the courts or through their deaths, we have little knowledge about the thousands of men who passed through Dorchester between 1914 and 1919, nor what they thought about their captives. No lists of names survive and the few records to be found in the British or German archives tell us nothing about them. As for personal testimonies, I have found only a few, one of which provides the scantiest of information.

One remarkable man who did record some very interesting information about his short stay at the camp was Gunther Plüschow, distinguished as being the only person in either WW1 or WW2 to escape from this country and get back to Germany, and his story might have come straight from the pages of the *Boy's Own Paper*. When the War began, Gunther was serving as a lieutenant pilot with the East Asian Naval Station at Tsingtau, a German enclave in China. The air station had only two aircraft and when one of them crashed, Gunther became the lone flyer. As a consequence of the outbreak

71 *Western Gazette*, 25/9/1914.
72 *Western Gazette*, 18/12/1918.

of war, on 15 August the Japanese served an ultimatum on the German government to leave Tsingtau, which was ignored. Accordingly, Japan declared war on Germany and began, jointly with a British force, to besiege the colony.

By November 1914, the military situation had become untenable, so, before the garrison fell, Plüschow was given the last military and diplomatic dispatches from the Governor and told to fly them to Germany in his much-repaired Taube aircraft. He had only gone about 160 miles when the plane crashed into a paddy field and, after setting fire to the machine, he set out on foot for his homeland. Somehow he managed to get a pass to travel across China and eventually arrived in the city of Nanking. There he got the distinct feeling that he was being watched by the authorities and just as he was about to be arrested he jumped into a rickshaw and went to the railway station, where he boarded a train to Shanghai, after bribing a guard. In Shanghai he met the daughter of a German diplomat he knew, who provided him with papers indicating that he was a Swiss national, together with money and a ticket for a ship heading for San Francisco.

He arrived in the USA in January 1915, then crossed the country to New York City. Again, he was fortunate enough to meet someone he knew, a friend who got him travel documents for a ship sailing to Italy. It was on this trip that his luck failed him when, because of bad weather, the ship put in at Gibraltar, where he was arrested by the British. His identity was revealed and he was sent to England, where he spent a short time in Dorchester before moving on to the officer camp at Donnington Hall.

Gunther Plüschow, the only man in either World War to escape from Britain and return to Germany. (Source: Plüschow.)

It was from Donnington Hall that Gunther made his escape, making his way to London, where he hatched his plan for getting back to Germany. He decided to take on the character of an English dock worker and travel to Tilbury, where he would attempt to board a foreign ship heading for a neutral country. After several attempts, including one where he almost drowned, he managed to board a ship which took him to the Netherlands, from whence he returned to Germany. Having arrived in his homeland he was promptly arrested as a spy, nobody believing that anyone could have made such a journey, but once his identity was established he was proclaimed a hero, decorated and received a promotion.

That was by no means the end of his adventures. After the War, and after several jobs, he joined the crew of a sailing ship bound for South America and, after signing off, travelled overland across Chile to Patagonia. In 1927 he returned to Chile and began flying again with Ernst Dreblow, the two of them being the first to explore by air the Cordillera Darwin mountain range and the Southern Patagonian ice field. When Gunther returned to Germany he wrote a book and produced a documentary film about his explorations; then, the following year he went back to Patagonia with Dreblow to continue his explorations. It was there, in 1931, that the two men were killed when their plane crashed near Lake Argentino.

Plüschow wrote a book about his war-time experiences, in which he described his brief stay in Dorchester. Before arriving in the town, he had been kept, along with other German prisoners, on the Cunard ship *Andania*, where he was very unhappy about his treatment. His arrival in Dorchester and his comments on the camp and its staff are best described in his own words.

> 'In the evening we reached Dorchester, where I was greeted by a totally different atmosphere. An English Captain (whose name was Mitchell) from the prisoners' of war camp approached me and asked politely whether I was an officer.
>
> "Yes," I replied.
>
> "In that case I am surprised that you should have been brought to a soldiers' camp. Please forgive me if I cannot have you escorted by an officer. But my senior Sergeant-Major will come with you. Will you kindly walk alone behind the other prisoners?"
>
> I was speechless. As we were marching through this delightful, clean little town, I suddenly heard "The Watch on the Rhein"[73] being sung behind us loudly, gaily and with zest, followed by the most beautiful soldier songs, and then "O Germany, High in Honours!" We thought we were dreaming, but when we looked round in amazement we saw a group of about fifty German soldiers who had been commandeered from the camp to the station to collect our luggage.
>
> Oh how our hearts beat! In the midst of enemies, in spite of wounds and captivity, this flaming enthusiasm, this rapturous singing! I must admit that

73 De Wacht am Rhein (The Guard or Watch on the Rhine) was a popular patriotic song based on traditional enmity between the Germans and the French. In its report of 5 August 1917, the *Milwaukee Journal* claimed that the song had been banned in the Dorchester camp.

the English were extraordinarily tolerant, and the population always behaved in exemplary fashion. Silently, closely pressed together, they stood on both sides of the street. From all the windows fair little heads peeped at us, but not one contemptuous gesture, not one abusive word. They even seemed to enjoy listening to the German melodies.

In camp thirty civilian prisoners were allotted a small wooden hut, which combined our bed, dining and sitting room. A tiny palliasse, which lay on the floor, and two blankets made up our sleeping accommodation. My Captain begged me to put up with existing conditions, as he was unfortunately unable to give me a special room to myself.

The Camp at Dorchester contained 2000 to 3000 prisoners and consisted of an old race-horse stables and of wooden barracks.[74] The prisoners were extremely comfortable, as the food was good, plentiful and the treatment irreproachable, and there were many opportunities for sport.

I left my hut and moved into a small room over the stables, where I was warmly received by Sergeant Major N. Life in this room was unique and full of intimate comradeship. My colleagues were, apart from N, a huge Bavarian infantry soldier of the Body Guards Regiment, whose nickname was "Schorsch",[75] and who acted as our cook; a nimble and clever private in the Hussars from Lorraine, a policeman by profession; and also two splendid rifle guards of gigantic stature, genuine blond Frisians. After a week we received a seventh guest. This was the sub-lieutenant H, the observer whom the English had fished out of the North Sea with his pilot, after they had been floating about on the wrecked machine for over forty hours.

The comradeship in this room was ideal. The men had all been taken at the great retreat of the Maine,[76] and, as was expected, these splendid fellows had only fallen into the enemy's hands when severely wounded. They were of such fine disposition, and showed such burning love for their country, that my heart filled with pride and satisfaction. The evenings were especially pleasant. We contrived a rough game with a board and some pieces of cork, and gambled on petits chevaux,[77] regularly every night, with childish delight.

Every afternoon 400 to 800 prisoners, of course closely guarded by English soldiers, were led out for their exercise into lovely open country. I often accompanied them. All the time our soldier songs were sung, but with particular force and ecstasy when we marched through the town, going and returning. "The Watch on the Rhein" and "O Germany, High in Honours!" Imagine 300 or 400 of our picked men, our victorious troops under General von Kluck! The English

74 Plüschow seems not to have known that the stables belonged to the Royal Horse Artillery Barracks.

75 A form of the name George.

76 He probably means the German retreat at the Battle of the Marne, in September 1914.

77 Little Horses, a gambling board game.

population behaved even then with the utmost restraint, and never uttered a word of abuse or threat.

The sergeant-major told me of a very nice episode. When Major Owen and Captain Mitchell were appointed to the camp, their wives implored them not to go among the "Huns" without escort and without being heavily armed. The two old soldiers, however, kept their own counsel, and were not devoured! After a time they suggested to their wives that they should visit the camp and convince themselves that the German soldiers were quite normal people and not monsters as portrayed in the press. Naturally, at first, the ladies fainted away. But after much persuasion, and being assured of a bodyguard, they ventured upon entering their husbands' offices and watched the doings of the German soldiers. The news of the visit got about, and silently our male choir assembled under the windows and warbled forth its finest songs. I am told that the ladies were so deeply moved that they were unable to speak, and could not hold bitter tears. From thence onwards they often came and showed our men much kindness.

Another story is also typical. A new Colonel came to the camp. On the first round he was armed to the teeth, and walked about between two soldiers, with fixed bayonets, one in front and the other behind him. When he met the Major and the Captain, absolutely unarmed and unaccompanied, he reproached them severely for their carelessness. But he soon improved.

One day this new Commandant sent for these two gentlemen and said to them in a tone of horror, "Can you imagine this? We have been sent some new prisoners and it has been reported that they are full of lice. Such dreadful things can only happen to the Germans."

Captain Mitchell turned calmly to the Major.

"Do you remember Owen that we were so covered with lice during the last campaign that we simply could not move?"

The Colonel was aghast. I must point out that though the Colonel was a Colonel he had never in his life had anything to do with military affairs. But that can only happen in England.'[78]

The identity of one of the prisoners of war was revealed to me by a remarkable coincidence. I was asked by Southern Television to help produce a short programme about the Dorchester camp as part of their anniversary commemorations for the beginning of the War. A few weeks after the broadcast, I received a telephone call from a woman who lived in Corfe Mullen in East Dorset, saying that a friend of hers had been watching the item when one of the photographs I had provided appeared on the screen. There, standing at the front of the group of other prisoners, was her godfather, Johann Baur.

---

78 Plüschow.

The lad, for he looks but a boy, came from Rot bei Laupheim, Baden Wurttemberg, where his extended family farmed. Johann was captured at the beginning of the War and appears to have had a happy time during his stay in England, where, as he told his goddaughter, the local population were kind to him. He remembered being taken to the seaside, probably Weymouth, and on one occasion he was given 'high tea', not just tea and cakes but also ham and cheese. Like most of his fellow captives from southern Germany, Johann was a Roman Catholic and performed in the camp choir at religious services and on social occasions.

Johann Baur taking soup from the kitchen to his comrades.(Courtesy of the Keep Military Museum.)

After 4 years away from home, the young soldier who returned to his family was not the same person who left them. The area of Germany where he lived was, and still is, noted for its conservatism and what many consider outdated views on gender roles. So, it was quite a shock to his family when he put on an apron and cooked, did the washing up or helped clean the house, all things he had picked up during his stay in the camp. Johann's goddaughter remembers that she never heard him speak English after he returned home, until 1955 that is. In that year she and her husband and daughter, who were then living in Dorset, went to see their German relatives. One day, she heard her husband talking to someone in another room, in English, and was surprised to find that it was Johann. In the course of conversation he asked her if she knew a place called Dorchester where he had been a POW. His goddaughter was able to tell him that her daughter was born there.

Another German soldier who found himself in Dorchester was Georg Ludwig Prell. Born in April 1885 in Wunsiedel, Upper Franconia, in the north-east of Bavaria, Georg's military pass book indicates that he joined the German Army on 21 October 1905, serving with the 4th Coy of the 6th Infantry Regiment. In 1906 he was promoted to the rank of lance-corporal and just 1 month later rose to sergeant. It appears that he then left the army and rejoined on 1 April 1913. Georg was captured sometime between July and November 1916, during the Battle of the Somme, and was sent to Dorchester, where he sat out the rest of the War. Back home, like British women, his wife Julia was doing her bit to aid the war effort, working as a post woman. Georg was discharged from the military in 1919.

Left: this photograph of Georg Prell was taken by Charles Furbear, photographer of 36 Great Western Road. It was made into a postcard, which Georg sent to his brother Bernhardt. Right: Julia Prell in her post-woman's uniform, waiting at home, like thousands of wives, for her husband to return home. (Source: www.europeana1914-1918.eu (Horst Carstiuc).)

The evidence we have for Martin Pfleiderer's stay in Dorchester comes from a postcard he took back to Germany. The image portrayed on it is of the Camp Commandant, Col Bulkeley. Martin was born on 24 July 1896 in the small town of Winnenden, 15 miles north-east of Stuttgart. He was captured at Ypres in May 1916, after he had been

Martin Pfleiderer, third from the right, back row, posing with a group of comrades. (Source: www.europeana1914-1918.eu (Traugot Pfleiderer).)

seriously injured. After spending a short while in Southampton, Martin was transferred to Dorchester and then returned home, via Switzerland, as part of a prisoner exchange. After the War he studied theology and worked as a protestant pastor from 1936 to 1961.

Johann Baur, Georg Prell and Martin Pfleiderer were among the majority of prisoners who served their confinement in quiet anonymity; however, like Gunther Plüschow, one man, named Bruno Schmidt-Reder, hit the national headlines in this country. Schmidt-Reder, a major in the German Army, was one of the captives taken off the *SS Potsdam* on 24 August 1914 in Falmouth. He was sent to Dorchester, where he spent a short period of time, before being repatriated to Germany as unfit for military service. He was suffering from a serious medical complaint at the time, which necessitated an operation. What he did when he got home provoked several questions in the House of Commons concerning the nature of his release and the Government's policy on exchanging prisoners.[79]

Mr Ronald O'Neill, Unionist MP for the St Augustine's Division of Kent, asked the Under-Secretary for War if he had knowledge of a pamphlet, published in Berlin, purportedly by Schmidt-Reder, describing his release from Dorchester. He was particularly alarmed by the fact that the pamphlet contained photographs of the inside of the camp, a breach of the rule that forbade prisoners from having photographic equipment. Further, it was possible that he had taken photographs of other places which could be of use to the enemy. That led to a supplementary question, asking if the prisoner had been searched before his release. The Under-Secretary said that he did not know because the senior officers of the camp had been changed since his removal. Another MP was more concerned at the fact that a German prisoner had been repatriated without being exchanged for a British POW. He was informed that it was normal practice for men under the age of 17 and over 55, doctors and ministers of the church to be released without reciprocation.

Schmidt-Reder did publish a pamphlet in Germany about his experiences of being captured and his subsequent release.[80] It does, indeed, contain four photographs depicting scenes in and around the camp, but it is most unlikely that Schmidt-Reder took them. They were most probably some of the many taken by local photographers and made available for sale, usually as postcards.

---

79 House of Commons Parliamentary Debates.
80 Schmidt-Reder.

In the pamphlet he wrote poetically about the lovely scenery around the camp, describing the green slopes, rising gently toward the ancient hill fort. He was amazed by the beautiful sunsets, which he claimed were better than any he had seen in the tropics, and added that even the most unappreciative person could not fail to be impressed by the work of art provided by the colours.

Inside the camp he noted that there were some very old and fine horse chestnut trees under which, on Sunday afternoons, a Scottish protestant pastor, probably the Rev Holmes, held services for a large audience. After a short sermon, the pastor asked his congregation what song they would like to sing. 'Naturally,' he says, 'De Wacht am Rhein,' a popular patriotic song of the time, based on enmity between the Germans and the French. He claims that the singing spread throughout the camp until every German was singing it, something that, if it were true, must have been intimidating for the soldiers guarding the camp. However, the balance was maintained when the pastor suggested that they finished the service by singing 'God Save the King'. According to Schmidt-Reder, the pastor made the plight of the prisoners less stressful.

Drawing by prisoner E. Streuber done in 1919 entitled Unter Den Kastanien (Under the Horse Chestnut Trees). These are the trees under which Rev Holmes held religious services for Lutheran prisoners. (Courtesy of the Keep Military Museum.)

Rev Holmes made his contribution towards the well-being of his flock in the camp, but there were a whole range of factors, mostly under the control of the Commandant and his staff, that affected their physical and psychological health.

Food

When a person is imprisoned for a long period of time, everyday things take on a new significance. Gunther Plüschow explained how receiving letters became a central focus of prison camp life, and the same could be said of food, which not only maintained physical health but also contributed towards the psychological well-being of the individual and the morale of the prisoners as a whole. Meal times gave structure to the prisoner's day and for those with time on their hands it helped relieve the monotony of their existence. Familiar items sent from home in parcels gave comfort and provided a tangible connection with the Fatherland. Food also provided a focal point of discussion and something to moan about with one's friends.

The arrangements for rationing prisoners of war were set out in the Hague Convention, but the details were vague. Basically, it said that in the absence of an agreement between belligerent nations, prisoners of war were to receive the same rations as soldiers of the holding country. This ignored the fact that not all soldiers got the same ration. A British soldier stationed in the Depot, for instance, got different rations than the fighting soldier. Food and rationing became a contentious issue between governments and was a convenient weapon to use in the propaganda war, especially in the early years when, because of unpreparedness, camps were not equipped to deal with the unexpectedly large numbers of prisoners. Germany and Britain did not agree a mutual food standard but established their own.

In British camps the daily ration was provided free of charge and in 1914 it consisted of:

1 lb 8 oz of bread or 1 lb of biscuits
8 oz of fresh meat or 4 oz of pressed meat ('Bully')[81]
1 oz of tea
1 oz of coffee
2 oz of sugar
1-lb tin of condensed milk
8 oz of fresh vegetables
Pepper
2 oz of cheese or 1 oz of butter
2 oz of beans, lentils or rice.

81 Bully, or Bully Beef (from the French *boeuf bouilli*), was similar to corned beef. Brisket of beef was cured, minced, mixed with gelatine and then canned.

In the case of officer prisoners things were different. Initially, they too were fed for free, but after the German Government made a decision that British officers should pay for their food, a reciprocal decision was made regarding German officers. Additionally, officers could pay for a better diet. In the Donnington Hall camp they were paying 2 shillings a day for this typical menu:

Breakfast: Porridge, cod steaks, bread and butter.
Lunch: Cold meats, fried potatoes, beetroot salad, bread and butter.
Dinner: Vienna steaks, onions, beans, mashed potatoes, and pancakes.

Signing herself as 'An Englishwoman', one person was in no doubt about the quality of the food being served up to German officers, when she wrote to the *London Times*, 'The contrast between the luxury of German prisoners in England and the misery of the English captives in Germany is most marked. Though it was said to be "impossible" for her to buy salmon in our town, my daughter recently discovered two fine fish in the back of the shop "for the German officers" and firmly insisted on buying some, much to the fishmongers' annoyance. Next week, though salmon was ordered specially, a small bit of head was sent her, everything of the best being saved for the Germans by the patriotic fishmonger! At another prisoners' camp the local butchers were informed when the camp was started that only prime cuts were to be supplied, with the result that the butchers' best customers living round the corner were obliged to put up with what was left.'[82]

The lady was not the only person to complain about the food provided to prisoners. In April 1917, a Northampton manufacturer appeared before a tribunal seeking permission to buy a jam boiler. He complained that the Government had commandeered all his jam for the German prisoners' camp, and his firm had none for the public. In reply, the Chairman of the tribunal replied, 'That's just what they do; exactly what you might expect! Of course the German prisoners must have jam. I shall not be surprised if they commandeer all the foodstuff there is in the town. The Germans' camp must have first consideration.' Another member of the panel suggested, sarcastically, that the Government's generosity was one of the reprisals for the sinking of British hospital ships.[83]

In comparison with the British arrangements, the German Government did not set a defined ration but created a 'standard,' to be followed. British

82 *London Times*, 4/12/1914.
83 *Western Gazette*, 6/4/1917.

prisoners were to receive sufficient plain food, which in its composition and quantity was to be adapted to reflect the type of work being carried out. Prisoners were to receive the same quantity of bread as German troops in civilian quarters. Three meals a day were to be served on the following basis:

> 'In the morning: Coffee, tea or soup.
> At noon: A plentiful fare consisting of meat and vegetables. The meat may be replaced by a correspondingly larger portion of fish.
> At night: A substantial and plentiful meal.'[84]

In British camps, regulations stipulated that personnel involved in the ordering, preparation and cooking of food should be properly trained. Those involved in ordering food supplies, the NCOs who organised the kitchens and those who cooked were required to undergo a week's training. The responsibility for ensuring that the prisoners were fed properly every day was undertaken by a kitchen committee, appointed by the Camp Commandant, on which served, among others, the camp surgeon and the person responsible for ordering stores. It was their responsibility to ensure the quality and appropriateness of the diet, in regard to nutrition, freshness and the needs of the prisoners, ensuring that, where possible, the prisoners' tastes were met and religious requirements were catered for. Any food that was deemed to be adulterated had to be sent to a laboratory for analysis. Camp medical officers, in the case of Dorchester Maj. Burrough Cosens, had the added burden of reporting any deficiencies in the provision to the commandant and ensuring that they were rectified. If he failed to do so he would be held responsible for any harm to the prisoners as a result of poor food.

Fortunately, we have a very detailed account of feeding arrangements in the Dorchester camp, during the summer of 1916. This is provided by a report by a Dr Taylor, of the American Embassy, who visited Dorchester between 20 and 26 August with the specific remit of inspecting the diet of the prisoners. At that time the camp was catering for 2,450 prisoners in four camp kitchens. The official arrived unannounced and stated that 'I was given every facility for personal investigation of the diet, from the initial delivery of the foodstuffs up to the point of completed preparation of the daily food of the prisoners of war. I was also given freedom to communicate with the

---

84 *The Treatment of Prisoners of War in England and Germany During the First Eight Months of the War*, HMSO, 1915.

German sergeants, kitchen chiefs and cooks, who were advised that I came from the American Embassy and that they were at liberty to present to me all complaints, suggestions or desires that they or the men might have.'[85]

During the week of his visit the investigator weighed each item of foodstuffs and found that they complied with the Government's specification. He noted that, to account for the possibility of fraud, each item of food was carefully counted and weighed when it was delivered to the camp, and was again checked by designated prisoners when it was handed to the kitchen chief and the German cooks, who ran the kitchens throughout the life of the camp. On inquiry, the men stated that at no time had the food allocated to them been less than what was required.

The investigator reported that a close eye was kept on the quality of the food, especially meat. Any concerns about standards were referred to Capt. Mitchell and subject to a joint inspection, to which the surgeon of the camp was usually called. Frozen beef, from Argentina, was received in the kitchens by a man who had formerly been a butcher by trade in Germany, who stated that occasionally the meat would show signs of decomposition and, in such cases, was rejected. He also commented that Capt. Mitchell and the medical officer, Dr Cousins, had strict ideas of quality. By the time of the visit the standard ration had been amended. Fish had been added but the cheese and butter had disappeared, the latter replaced by margarine. The portion 8 oz of fresh vegetables, usually cabbage, was served just once a week. In Dorchester the prisoners were receiving soup on 4 days of the week, served with legumes (i.e. beans and lentils) and meat, thickened with breadcrumbs. On 2 days meat was served, roasted or as goulash, and on Friday there was fish, nearly always salted herring. It was observed by the inspector that the situation regarding the small ration of fresh vegetables must have been difficult for many of the prisoners who came from peasant families and ate mainly vegetables. Fresh fruit seemed to be entirely absent from the ration, although the inspector was impressed with the variety of fruit and vegetables which could be bought in the canteen.

Each row of prison huts had its own kitchen, where the food was cooked in large coal-fired stoves by German chefs, overseen by a German NCO. The prepared food was then taken by orderlies to the huts, where it was eaten. One complaint made by those working in the kitchens was that they were required to bring in the coal for the stoves. This they regarded as an excessive burden, pointing out also that it was impossible to keep their kitchen clothing

85 Report to the British Government dated 23 September 1916.

One of the camp kitchens, showing the coal-fired cauldrons and ovens. (Courtesy of the Keep Military Museum.)

clean when they were required to carry coal every day. The problem was solved by appointing coal orderlies.

Dr Taylor noted that breakfast in the camp was served at 7 am, dinner at midday and supper at 4 pm. Morning and evening meals consisted of coffee, with condensed milk, and bread and margarine. The remainder of items included in the Government's diet were served at the noon meal, including the meat, vegetables, beans, lentils and potatoes. In fact, in the Dorchester camp the men were given 10 oz of potatoes, rather than 8, the additional 2 oz being paid for by profits from the camp canteen. Whilst potatoes were being fed to prisoners, it appears that not everyone was happy with the situation. Member of Parliament

Following a complaint by the prisoners that this soup was too thin the cooks were replaced. Presumably this photograph was taken after the change was made. (Courtesy of the Keep Military Museum.)

Capt. Angus Hambro[86] felt obliged to complain to Capt. Bathurst,[87] in the House of Commons that potatoes were being supplied to German prisoners that were unobtainable by the public. Bathurst promised to draw the attention of the Agricultural War Committee to such an undesirable use of potatoes.

The American inspector's verdict on Dorchester was that the diet provided by the basic ration was 'adequate, competent, of good quality and well prepared.'[88] However, the report did contain some criticisms and suggestions. One of the main criticisms was that because the Government ration was applied so strictly by the War Office, it gave the Camp Commandant no freedom to obtain any equivalent items from local markets. Doing so would have provided a more varied diet and, perhaps, saved money. Beef was the meat of choice at the camp and it seems that the prisoners were finding it monotonous at every meal, so they requested the inspector to ask if they could have pork or mutton once a week.

Another problem highlighted lay with those prisoners who left the camp to work, particularly those who did heavy labour, like quarrying or logging. These men had breakfast in the camp and then either took their midday meal with them or were sent it, later returning to eat supper with the rest of the prisoners. Thus, despite doing a hard day's work they received exactly the same ration as those who did not work. The exception were those prisoners who were employed by farmers who fed them, in accordance with an agreement with the camp Camp Commandant. These men often got better food than those in the camp. This situation regarding work and diet was recognised by the Camp Commandant in 1918, who, when asked if he could provide prisoners for road building, stated that they barely received enough nourishment to do light work let alone heavy manual work.[89]

In some of the German POW camps British prisoners were permitted to buy half a litre of beer and a quarter litre of wine several times weekly, provided it was drunk where it was bought and not sold to other prisoners. This was not the case in British camps, where only officers were allowed to buy alcohol. Clearly, Other Ranks were not to be trusted. This did not stop the Dorchester prisoners putting in a request to the commandant for alcohol to be made available. Dr Taylor was on the side of the prisoners, saying, 'In the opinion of the writer this request is reasonable and no real objections to

86 Angus Valdemar Hambro, MP for South Dorset (1910–1922) and North Dorset (1937–1945).

87 Charles Bathurst, 1st Viscount Bledisloe, GCMG, KBE, PC, (1867–1958), Secretary for Food.

88 Report to the British Government dated 23 September 1916.

89 Jones.

it are apparent. The Germans are a beer-drinking people. Confinement in a POW camp is at best a wearing situation. The use of beer and wine in such quantities stands, in the opinion of the writer, upon the same footing as the use of tobacco.'[90] To his credit, Maj. Bulkeley declared that he agreed with the complaints and suggestions, including the provision of alcohol, and said he would do what he could to change things. The prisoners never did get their beer, because of Government policy.

One item that the prisoners seem to have little complaint about was bread, despite early disappointments. Initially, this item was baked outside the camp by local bakers, but there were complaints, entirely justifiable, that it was not cooked through. Consequently, the commandant asked for permission for a bakery to be built within the camp. This request was acceded to and by the end of 1914 the prisoners were baking enough bread to keep their comrades happy. The German bakers must have been baking around the clock in order to provide bread for around 3,000 people every day. And happy it seems the prisoners were, one declaring that the bread was 'as good as cake'.[91] At one stage the prisoners asked if they could have pumpernickel, the heavy rye bread loved by Germans, but the commandant had to refuse because of the difficulty of getting rye.

Coffee was a great favourite with the German prisoners and there certainly seemed to be no shortage of it. One visitor to the camp commented that 'Coffee is provided in enormous quantities, and judging from a cup enjoyed by the correspondent, is better prepared than the beverage retailed under that name in any but the best restaurants in London.'[92]

Equally effusive was another visitor, Mr Kettleston, London correspondent of the Norwegian newspaper *Aftenposten*, who visited the camp in December 1915. He compared the plight of those in the camp to their countrymen back home, writing, 'These German prisoners did not need, like their free bretheren in Germany, tickets for meat, butter and bread. No, the meat, butter and bread that they got were of the best quality and were handed to them in ample quantity.'[93] As the war progressed the British civilian population began to experience food shortages, to a large degree brought about by the German policy of unrestricted sinking of merchant ships, introduced in 1915. By August 1917 the diet in the camp had changed again, reflecting the new situation. The bread ration was reduced from the original 24 oz to 13 oz

90 Report to the British Government dated 23 September 1916.
91 *Chronicle*, 23/12/1915.
92 *Reading Eagle*, 23/1/1916.
93 *Calgary Herald*, 19/2/1916.

and the meat ration from 8 oz to 6 oz on 5 days of the week. On the other 2 days salt herring was provided. Fresh vegetables were confined to turnips. The amounts of tea, coffee and sugar were reduced, although the diet did have oatmeal, which was added to the flour to increase the bread ration. A small quantity of jam was added.

Another result of the shortage of imported goods was the disappearance of some items from the camp canteen. From February 1917, items containing sugar, jam, syrup, flour, as well as meat and game were no longer permitted to be sold in canteens, or otherwise made available for prisoners to buy.

By the end of 1918 the ration looked a lot different from the original. The bread ration was just 9 oz per day, although 4 oz of broken biscuit was added. Another new arrival on the menu was horse meat, which was served on 3 days of the week. Bacon was available on 2 days and salt-cured or smoked herrings on Friday. Oatmeal, maize, split-peas and more beans were added, the latter apparently replacing fresh vegetables. Panayi suggests that the above ration was given only to those prisoners who were employed and that those not working got less. For example, their bread ration was just 5 oz and they received less rice, oatmeal, cheese, margarine and maize than those who were working.

One very popular facility in the camp was the canteen. It was run on a profit-making basis by the prisoners and provided an important source for

The canteen was very popular with the prisoners, where they could buy many items that made life a little easier. Only officers were allowed to buy alcohol. (Courtesy of the Keep Military Museum.)

additions to the basic diet. When Mr Van de Veer visited in December 1915, he found 'an excellent canteen, where for very little money prisoners buy non-alcoholic drinks, fruit, cigarettes, tobacco, etc.' One of the few things that has survived from the camp is a notice, which was displayed in the canteen, showing the list of things that were available to buy in April 1919, 5 months after the end of the War. Food items included dried and tinned apples, various cakes, cheese, butter, chocolate, custard powder, eggs, a variety of dried fruit, jams, macaroni and tinned rabbit, but the favourite item was undoubtedly German sausages, which were disappearing from the shelves at the rate of between 500 and 1,000 lb per week.

Another useful and eagerly awaited source of food was the parcel from home. It was a huge morale booster, made a physical connection to one's loved ones and provided favourite foods. Again, German sausage was a common content, as were dried fruit, cake and tobacco. Like the standard ration, the contents of food parcels altered, reflecting food shortages in Germany, which became chronic in 1918.

Supplying food to prisoners by the civilian population, other than where there was an agreement that an employer should provide meals for working prisoners, was an offence against the Defence of the Realm Act and the law was enforced strictly. The view taken was that supplying food to the prisoners not only could facilitate escape but also was likely to interfere with discipline and administration in the place of detention. All bakers, for example, were warned by the police of the heavy penalties for giving or selling bread to prisoners. There were certainly plenty of opportunities for the sympathetic or enterprising person to supply food, particularly in rural areas like Dorset, where POWs worked on remote farms and, although under guard, were not always closely guarded. Despite the severe penalties, there were some contraventions of this law involving local civilians and prisoners of war.

One such case concerned Thomas Greenwood, a baker from Manswood, Moor Critchel, who appeared before the Wimborne magistrates on Friday 17 May 1918, accused of supplying a quantity of bread, namely six-and three-quarters loaves, to prisoners working in the neighbourhood. The chief witness was one of the guards whom, as if to add credence to his statement, the *Western Gazette*[94] pointed out was wearing a wound stripe and two good conduct chevrons. He stated that he had occasion to leave the prisoners for just a minute or two, although he kept his eye on them all the time, and, on returning, he found Mr Greenwood supplying them with bread.

94 *Western Gazette*, 24/5/1918.

Compounding the felony, he pointed out that the accused had earlier in the day refused to serve a person who had five little children and whose husband was a POW in Germany. In answer to a question, the guard replied that the defendant could not have mistaken the prisoners for English men because of their uniforms and the fact that they spoke very little English. Greenwood, who pleaded guilty, stated that on coming from the house of a customer he found his bread cart surrounded by German prisoners. They asked him for bread, but he told them to move on, which they did not do. He claimed that he did not know what to do with them and, after being pressed, sold them the loaves for 1 s 6 d to get rid of them. Just as he was handing over the loaves the guard came around the corner and saw what was going on. He pointed out that the prisoners, who had been working in the village for 2 years, were free to roam about and had never caused any trouble. The magistrates took a particularly dim view of this case because of the shortages being endured by the civilian population at the time, and, consequently, Greenwood was sentenced to 6 months' hard labour in Dorchester Gaol and fined £25. His appeal against the verdict at the next Quarter Sessions was refused.

Another baker who got into trouble was William Barnes of Puddletown, a village 5 miles east of Dorchester. He appeared at a sitting of Dorchester Magistrates Court, which was chaired by Mr Alfred Pope, the brewer, at the Shire Hall on Saturday 24 August 1918. Barnes and his 17-year-old son Frederick were summoned for selling bread and flour to a POW. The first witness to appear was Pte Charles Chalice of the RDC, who stated that while performing his duties as escort to six German prisoners of war, three at Walter Kingman's Norris Mill Farm and three at Thomas Kingman's Duddle Farm, Puddletown, he found a prisoner in a barn at Norris Mill smuggling out a paper bag of flour. The flour had been hidden in a trough on a beam and the prisoner was in the act of removing it when he spotted the guard and ran off to a nearby stable, followed by Pte Chalice, who challenged him, took possession of the flour and went back to the barn, where he found two loaves. Returning to the prisoner he told him that he would have to report what he had found. The prisoner said, 'If you report me, the baker will get into trouble,' and begged him not to, adding, 'The baker has been a good friend to us.'[95] Despite these pleas the offending items were handed over to the civil police, which took up the investigation. P.C.s Payne and Slow were despatched and caught up with Barnes and his son at Tincleton, on their rounds. On being questioned, the son admitted supplying a small loaf for 9 d

95 *Somerset County Herald and Taunton Courier*, 28/8/1918.

to the prisoner, but not the large one. The father, in the first instance, denied selling anything, but later admitted that he had sold a large loaf and the flour to the prisoner, and said in mitigation that he had heard that the prisoners were given extras, such as a cup of tea or a plate of bread and butter by the Kingmans. P.C. Snow told the court that he had, on a previous occasion, gone to Barnes and warned him that he was not to give the prisoners anything.

The baker Barnes pleaded that he had no desire to facilitate the 'Huns' escape and when he offered the loaf to the prisoner he expected him to eat it on the spot. He also said that there had been numerous occasions when, during his round, prisoners had offered to buy bread from him and he had always refused. His son Frederick pleaded the same defence as Greenwood in the previous case, that there was no way that he could have known that the loaf he sold was to one of the German prisoners, as he was wearing normal civilian clothes and spoke like an Englishman. There then followed quite a debate about whether the Kingmans supplying the prisoners with additional food was against the law or not. Despite Barnes' plea of innocence, he was fined £50 and informed that the sentence could have been one of 6 months' imprisonment. The younger Barnes was bound over to keep the peace.

Not all cases were about food. One brought before the Dorchester Bench in January 1915 involved an item that, far from facilitating an escape, was more likely to impede it. Once again, P.C. Payne was in the thick of the action, this time at Woodsford, a village close to Puddletown. On the afternoon of 10 December 1914, Payne, along with another constable, was watching the cottage of a Mrs House, presumably after a tip-off, when they saw a German prisoner going in. A little boy was then seen to leave the building carrying a big bag with something in it. Soon after, the prisoner who had been working at a nearby farm belonging to a Mr Paul, emerged from the cottage with something in his pockets which caused them to bulge. On being stopped and searched he was found to have two bottles of port wine in his possession.

Payne took the wine into the cottage and asked Mrs House if she could account for how they were in the prisoner's possession. She replied, 'Yes, I let them have them. They paid me 30 shillings.' Later she admitted that she had sold German prisoners seven bottles of port wine for 50 shillings, the balance being carried by the young boy in the bag. When told that she would be reported she retorted, 'It is hard, you cannot supply a German with anything. They are human. I admit I have let them have bread, cigarettes, and milk, but someone don't like it, and have put you on my track. Never mind, I do it openly, but some of them do it on the sly; but I will show them up.'[96] Mrs House accepted the charge of supplying the port wine to the prisoners, but pleaded not guilty of selling it to them without a licence and asked the magistrates to be lenient with her on account of her having eight children all under the age of sixteen. She was told that she had committed a serious offence and was given the option of paying a fine of £10 or serving 2 months' imprisonment. She elected to pay the fine, plus another £10 for selling alcohol without a licence. One wonders how many cases of food and drink being sold to prisoners remained undetected.

96 *Western Gazette*, 10/1/1915.

Health and Pastoral Care

Some of the local newspapers, reporting on the arrival of early batches of prisoners in Dorchester, commented on how healthy they looked. The responsibility for keeping them that way whilst they were incarcerated in the camp fell to Dr William Burrough Cosens.

Cosens registered as a doctor in 1887 and worked for a period in Taunton, before coming to the County Hospital in Dorchester, where he was employed as honorary surgeon and played a leading role in raising subscriptions for a new operating theatre. He became a county magistrate and took a leading role in Dorchester's affairs, particularly during the War. In 1920, when the town got into protracted discussions about an appropriate form of war memorial, it was Cosens who lobbied for the monument we see in South Street today. On the outbreak of war he became honorary medical director for the British Red Cross Society in Dorset, and his first job was to devise a plan to co-ordinate the voluntary detachment medical services throughout the county. Locally, his remit covered the running of the town's three VAD[97] hospitals and organising the transfer of wounded from the railway stations to the hospitals. Soon after he took a commission with the RAMC and became medical officer for the prison camp.

The *Western Gazette* of 21 August 1914 reported on Cosens' appointment as medical officer at the camp and informed its readers that baths were being provided for the internees, and that a strict cleanliness regime was in place. Prisoners were required to wash their own underclothes and those who had no change of linen were provided with it. The *Gazette* added that 'The prisoners are likely to improve in physical condition.' This description contrasts somewhat with the findings of a report compiled by a Hamburg company after inspections of a number of camps in Britain. The Dorchester camp was visited in November 1914 and there were complaints that it was unclean and that there were only three baths and twelve basins for men to bathe in. The report also said that there was only one interpreter at the camp, who was unpleasant. The accuracy of these findings is difficult to establish; the inspections were, after all, made by representatives of the enemy whose

97 VAD or Voluntary Aid Detachments were formed in 1909 to provide volunteer assistance in times of war. During WW1 the majority of VAD personnel worked in hospitals in Britain and colonial countries. Of the 74,000 working in 1914, two-thirds were women or girls. Dorchester had three VAD hospitals. The main one was at Colliton House and the others were at 6 Church Street and the Freemasons' Hall in Princes Street. Colliton VAD is now used as a social club, 6 Church Street is a residence, and the Freemasons' Hall still maintains its original use.

visits came at a time when accusations and counter-accusations about the mistreatment of prisoners were common.[98] On the other hand, bearing in mind the great influx of prisoners into the camp during the first few months, it would have taken some time to build the necessary facilities and the visitors may have reported accurately.

Whatever the motives for the remarks, the British Government took them as serious concerns and steps were taken to improve matters. In February 1915, when Mr Jackson visited the camp, he was able to report that new toilet and wash-house facilities were being installed. Another visit to the camp took place in December 1915, this time by a member of the American Associated Press. At the time, there were just over 3,000 occupants and the correspondent observed that bath houses and laundries were liberally sprinkled over the camp. The bath houses were well equipped with showers and footbaths, for which an unlimited quantity of hot water was constantly supplied.[99]

On 20 August 1914 the *Chronicle* informed its readers that the health of the German prisoners would doubtless be improved by the 'pure breezes blowing over the grassy spaces of Poundbury'. Pure breezes they might be, but the hill fort over which the camp was extended is on an elevated, open site, with no protection from the elements. In the Government film of the camp, prisoners look decidedly cold when parading in the lower camp, but it was not for the want of warm clothing. In their report on the camp, Messrs Naville and Van Bercham commented that 'Nowhere need a prisoner complain of the cold by reason of tattered or insufficient clothing or want of boots. He has only to make representations and he will receive what he needs. It is a case of "all found". Civilian clothing is found for all, as the soldier's uniform is worn out.' The men were also provided with an overcoat, if necessary. The huts where the men were accommodated were built in sufficient numbers and size so that that there was never overcrowding in the camp, and each one was heated with flat iron stoves.

Establishing a healthy environment was one thing but maintaining it over a number of years was a more difficult task. New arrivals from the various theatres of war might bring in any manner of illnesses with them. On arrival at the camp each prisoner was medically examined to determine whether or not he had an infectious ailment, and if he did he

98 In the early period of the War both sides struggled to cope with the sudden influx of prisoners, leading to accusations of poor treatment and facilities. The number of accusations declined as the authorities got to grips with the situation.

99 *Reading Eagle*, 23/1/1916.

This photograph is entitled 'Airing the Bedding'. For health reasons the prisoners were encouraged to spend as much time as possible outside their huts and to air their bedding frequently. (Courtesy of the Keep Military Museum.)

was immediately isolated from the rest. Bedding was aired regularly and during the summer months the men were encouraged to spend as much time as possible in the open air.

One major preoccupation for those running the camp was the disposal of human waste produced by thousands of men each day. There are no records of any kind of a drainage system being installed when the camp was extended; however, there is a reference to men being employed to empty the latrines. Whatever method was used it seems that any major outbreak of disease caused by bad sanitation was kept at bay. The Norwegian Kittlesen exclaimed in 1917, after his visit to the camp, that the health of the prisoners was excellent, which could be seen from the fact that out of 3,408 prisoners, only 17 had been sent to the well-fitted-out hospital. He also said that there had never been an epidemic of any kind. The last report on the physical health of the internees came from Dr A. de Sturler and R. de Sturler in March 1919. They found that the prisoners' quarters were clean and well kept and all sanitary installations in good working order.

Whilst the majority of those taken prisoner were in good health and fit, many had sustained wounds, were suffering from the effects of gas or had been traumatised by battle. On 31 July 1916, among the 3,073 men present in the camp, 581 of them were wounded and waiting to be transferred to Switzerland. Depending on the severity of his wounds, a prisoner may be sent to one of the medical facilities inside or outside the camp. Within the camp the main medical facility was the former artillery camp hospital, which had a well-equipped operating theatre, dental surgery and dressing station, where patients who did not require actual hospital treatment went to have old wounds and injuries dressed, and received massage treatment. In December 1915 there were 20 men in this camp hospital, which had beds for 60, and in July 1916 the number was 21, with about 50 attending as outpatients.[100] They

100 Mark.

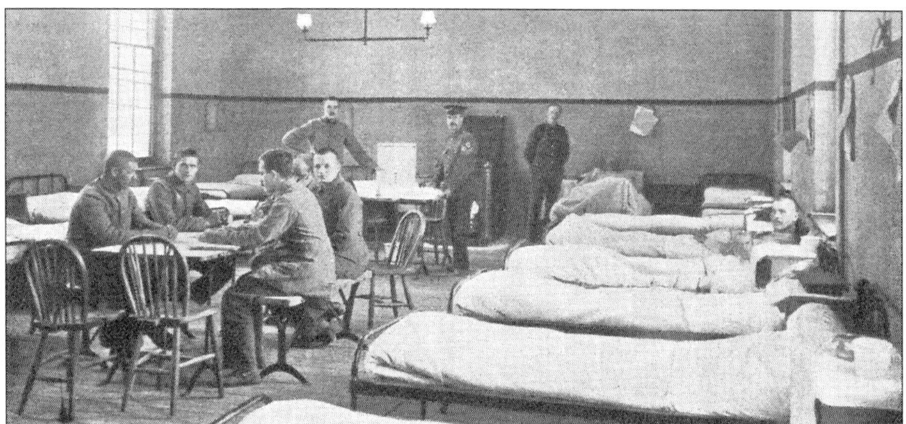

A ward in the artillery barracks hospital. (Courtesy of the Keep Military Museum.)

were being looked after by the camp doctors and a mixture of professional and VAD nurses, helped by medical orderlies.

By 1917 the medical facilities had increased considerably; as well as the brick-built hospital there were three hutted wards containing 112 beds. One of the huts was probably used as an isolation ward. During the year 1916, 377 cases were treated, many of whom had been severely wounded.[101] The

Medical staff and some patients pose outside the camp hospital. The German sitting on the left wears a Hussars uniform and an Iron Cross medal. (Courtesy of the Keep Military Museum.)

101 According to a visit by the Swiss legation on 26/3/1917.

most seriously wounded were often transferred to the County Hospital in Dorchester or even to the German Hospital in London.[102] The Swiss delegation's visit to the camp of 28 March 1919 noted that there were then 242 patients in the camp hospital; about 32 occupying the two wards in the building reserved for serious cases, while the majority of the lighter cases were accommodated in the huts. At that time there were only two severe cases being treated, one of nephritis and one of pulmonary tuberculosis. Both of the men were earmarked for repatriation.

This whimsical scene, outside the front of the camp hospital, shows the orderlies preparing for Christmas 1914. Each man has something to bring to the celebration, including the turkey, live in this case, carried by the cook. The unfortunate bird seems to be looking across to the person wielding the carving knife and fork. Note also the two black cats perched on the shoulders of two of the men. (Courtesy of the Keep Military Museum.)

Huts used as hospital wards were painted white and had large crosses on their gable ends.

There were a couple of occasions when the Dorchester authorities were caused some anguish by sick prisoners. The first case came to the attention of the Town Council's monthly meeting held in June 1915, when the Town Clerk read out a letter addressed to the Mayor. The sender was Denzil Hughes-Onslow, a prominent resident of the town who, together with his wife Marion, had moved out of their home, Colliton House, and allowed

102 The German Hospital, situated in Ritson Road, Dalston, East London, was founded in 1845 and offered free treatment to German-speaking immigrants. During WW1 the German staff remained at the Hospital, despite strong anti-German feelings from the local population.

Inside one of the three wooden huts used as hospital wards. The patients are wearing British Hospital Blues. VAD nurses have red crosses on their bibs, the others are regular nurses.

it to be used as a military hospital.[103] It had come to his attention that a German soldier, suffering from spotted fever,[104] had been transferred to the local Freemasons' Hall, which, as Onslow pointed out, was being used as a military hospital on the same basis as his own home for the treatment of wounded and sick allied servicemen. On the one hand, he was appalled that one of the enemy was being treated there and, on the other, he felt it 'monstrous' that someone with a highly infectious disease had been housed in the middle of the town, apparently without the knowledge of the town's Medical Officer of Health. As a rate payer he hoped that this occurrence would not happen again, especially because he understood that there was a strong feeling of indignation in the town that the Freemasons' Hall had 'now been rendered useless for the treatment of our own sick and wounded'.[105]

Onslow's letter caused considerable consternation among the councillors. Whilst some said that he was simply reflecting what others thought, others came to the defence of the hospital authorities, pointing out that the hall had since been thoroughly disinfected and was now ready to receive patients.

In September 1915 the case of two Austrian civilian prisoners led to some debate at a meeting of the Dorchester Board of Guardians, after two of them had been transferred to the County Lunatic Asylum. Under agreed

103 Denzil Hughes-Onslow, who had been offered the job of commanding the prison camp guard, declined the offer and instead was commissioned as a Major in the 6 Btn Dorset Rgt. He was killed on 10 July 1916 by a stray bullet whilst writing a dispatch in his dug-out.
104 Spotted fever was one of the many names given to typhus in the nineteenth century.
105 *Chronicle*, 10/6/1915.

arrangements, military prisoners requiring mental health care were to be charged to the War Department, but, in this case, because the men were civilian internees, the Army considered that they were the responsibility of the local authorities, under the Lunacy Acts. This was clearly a grey area and even the committee was divided about who should be responsible for them. The Clerk pointed out that as they were civilians in Dorchester the rules required that their cost should be shared between the Guardians and the Local Government Board. One member even suggested that as the men had been taken from a ship moored off the Isle of Wight it was the authorities there who should pay for them, and asked what would happen if another 50 internees sent to the camp had to be sent to the asylum. In the end they decided to ask the County Council to bear the cost.

Bearing in mind that thousands of men passed through the camp it is remarkable that in 5 years only 45 died. The first man to die was Bernhard Schneider, a 25-year-old soldier, on 28 August 1915. It appears that his death was the result of a terrible accident. An inquiry following his untimely end found that he had died as the result of accidental poisoning after he put carbolic acid into his bath as an antiseptic. It was at this inquiry that one of the German prisoners, Sgt Maj. Friedrich Kroger, the senior German NCO in the camp, felt obliged to make the following statement: 'I wish on behalf of the prisoners, and it is my duty, to say that the officers, medical staff, and NCOs did everything they could.' A week later he was buried and the *Chronicle* took the opportunity of reporting the event in great detail, in its own distinctive style:

> 'A military funeral is no uncommon sight in Dorchester, which has been for generations a garrison town and the quarters of various smart corps – of Royal Horse Artillery, field artillery, cavalry and infantry. But it is a spectacle which, by reason of the stately martial pomp and ceremonial which appeal to the eyes and of the solemn music and reverberating volleys which strike the ears never fails to attract a crowd of spectators. This is so in the "piping times of peace". But there was a special and novel interest in the military obsequies which on Tuesday morning lured hundreds of people from their beds at an earlier hour than usual, for it was the burial of the first German POW to die at the Dorchester Internment Camp. His name was Bernhard Schneider, his age 25, and he was physically a magnificent specimen of a man, considerably over six feet in height and superbly muscled. There is always something especially pathetic about a death in a strange land, where it is impossible for the deceased's kith and kin to stand by the graveside and bid the last farewell. In this instance, Bernhard Schneider, thanks to the consideration and liberal sentiments of the British military authorities, was

followed to the grave by a large and representative body of his compatriots and comrades-in-arms, and every usual honour done to deceased soldiers was duly and indeed punctiliously paid to this German soldier, this fallen foe buried in a foreign land.

The burial Service was begun at 6.15 am at the Prisoners of War Camp, in the place allotted to religious services. It was conducted in German with marked feeling and impressiveness by the Rev. R. Stratton Holmes, pastor of the Congregational Church, who is familiar with the language, and who, since the Prisoners of War Camp was established at Dorchester, has administered most acceptably to the Lutheran prisoners, and received many expressions of their grateful appreciation. All but the committal portion of the service was gone through at the Barracks, and any men in the Kriegsgefangenenlager (prisoner of war camp) who liked to attend were allowed to do so. There was a great crowd, and very beautiful the nodial[106] singing of a large choir.

The cortege left the Prisoners of War Camp, by Poundbury, on Tuesday at the early hour of 6.30 am, when the streets were nearly free of traffic; and the calm beauty of this perfect summer morning, with the pure sunlight shed upon fields and foliage, glossy with yet undispelled dew, seemed well to fit such a funeral. The solemn plaintive strains of the "Dead March" in Saul rising into the still morning air from the Prisoners of War Camp, announced to the crowd gathered by the Dorset Depot Barracks Citadel that the body had been brought out, and the funeral procession was about to issue forth. Shortly it appeared, and proceeded down High West Street towards Fordington churchyard, where the internment was to be made. The procession was preceded by two members of the Dorset Constabulary, clearing the way. Then came an officer of the Prison Guard and a firing party of seven files of National Reservists marching with arms reversed, followed by the Prison Guard brass band under bandmaster J. Honey, the drums draped in black.

The body, which was preceded by the officiating minister and undertaker (Mr Charles G. Wood),[107] was next borne on a gun-carriage and gun of the Royal Field Artillery, drawn by a team of horses preceded by a mounted NCO. The coffin plate was inscribed "Bernhard Schneider, died August 28th, aged 25". The coffin, draped with the German flag, was surmounted by floral tributes, including a handsome cross from the officers of the guard. Six of the deceased's comrades, acting as bearers, marched three on either side of the gun-carriage. This was followed by an open carriage conveying a large number of wreaths, some from British officers and men, as well as from the deceased's fellow soldiers. The men of every several company had sent a wreath with the words "Letzte Gruss" ("Last Greeting"). Upwards of 30 German soldiers, picked to represent various corps, were allowed to follow as

106 Poem or song of lamentation.
107 Woods Funeral Service is still operating in the town today.

mourners. Headed by the sergeant-major and accompanied by their Unter-Officieren[108] wearing distinguishing cap, these men, in the now familiar grey-green uniform, marched with typical Teutonic solidity, their measured heavy tread being very different from the march of English soldiers. One of the privates was observed to be wearing the Iron Cross. Colonel H. O'B. Owen, the officer commanding the Prisoners of War camp, and several of the senior officers followed, wearing mourning bands on their arms, and with them Dr W. Burrough Cosens, the medical officer in charge of the camp, and to whose skill and devotion the marvellous healthiness of the camp and health of the men must be attributed largely. Major Bulkeley was prevented by illness from attending; but he and Captain Mitchell had sent a wreath "with deepest sympathy". An escort of Wiltshire and Warwickshire National Reservists followed, with bayonets fixed and arms at the slope.

The Reservists band did not play down the High Street; and at the quick the procession proceeded along London Road to Grey's Bridge, and there turned the corner and reached Fordington St George's churchyard by Standfast Road, thus enabling the horses to avoid the steepness of Fordington Hill. When near the burial ground the slow march was resumed to renewed strains of the "Dead March" in Saul. The bearers carried in the coffin shoulder high, and the German soldiers, following two deep, carried each a wreath of flowers. They formed up on either side of the grave, which had been dug close to the immemorial yew tree. Here, most impressively, Mr. Holmes, amid the absolute stillness of the assembly, read the committal sentences; and to the words "Erde zu Erde, Staub zu Staub, Eschen zu Eschen" ("Earth to earth, ashes to ashes, dust to dust") the symbolic handfuls of "earth, dust and ashes" were thrown into the grave. At the close of the service the Lord's Prayer and the Blessing had been pronounced, the firing party discharged the three volleys over the open grave, and the bugler sounded the "Last Post". When the last dirge-like blast had died away the German prisoner mourners walked past the grave in single file and, according to German custom, each dropped a handful of earth upon the coffin. Prisoners and guard then reformed their ranks four deep and returned to the camp, the band playing a march at their head.

It was an interesting collection of floral tributes at the graveside. One wreath was inscribed, "From Colonel H. O'B. Owen, with sincere sympathy", and another, "From POW Hospital Camp, Dorchester". The funeral arrangements were carried out by Messrs Chas. G. Wood. He observed carefully the directions given by the Officer Commanding, whose sympathetic consideration, tact, and good dispositions in the matter must have been appreciated heartily by the comrades of the deceased. Fordington women are as plain-spoken as they are shrewdly observant; and one woman, looking on, gave expression to l'envoi

108 Non-Commissioned Officers.

(the last words), "I only hope that in Germany they treat our men as well and pay as much respect to those who die!"[109]

All of the prisoners that died in the Dorchester camp were buried in Fordington Cemetery, and, as time went on, the press reports of the funerals became less detailed. All but six of the dead, who were interred in the new part of the churchyard, were buried in the north section of the old churchyard, in a strip of land separated from the rest of the graves by a grass bank. Later ceremonies followed the same format as that of Schneider and every man was shown the same courtesies, and despite the early-morning start the people of the town always turned out in great numbers to watch the proceedings. After the burial a wooden cross was added to the grave indicating the man's name, age and regiment and this was later replaced by concrete headstones made by prisoners at the camp. In most instances two bodies were placed in the same plot. The Rev Holmes certainly officiated at several funerals, as did Father Hannigan, for the Catholic prisoners who died, but in some instances German personnel performed the duties. At the funeral of Carl Becker, for instance, the service was taken by a German Sergeant Major, whilst an officer officiated at the interment of Wilhelm Braun. In October 1919 the protestant minister officiating at Jakob Oeffler's funeral came from the camp.

Thomas Hardy was obviously affected by a visit to the prison hospital in September, 1916. He wrote: 'One prisoner, a Prussian, in much pain, died whilst I was with him – to my great relief and his own. Men lie helpless here from wounds; in the hospital 100 yards off other men, English, lie helpless from wounds – each scene of suffering caused by the other.'[110] Unfortunately, there is little information available about those who died, and what there is was recorded by the *Chronicle*. The newspaper reported that Alfred Hammel, aged 19, passed away in the County Hospital where he had been treated for an 'incurable malady', adding that he had received 'the skilled and kindly attendance of the medical and nursing staff'.[111] Emil Drygalla died at the County Hospital on 10 March 1916 after suffering from appendicitis, and Georg Meissner, who served with the 6th Reserve Infantry Btn, died of his wounds. Joseph Kohler and Ernst Zimmermann, a corporal, both died on New Year's Day 1919. Then there was Franz Radgowski who was shot by guards whilst trying to escape.

109 *Chronicle*, 2/9/1915.

110 Hardy. Thomas Hardy refers to Dorchester's main military hospital in Colliton House, Colliton Park.

111 *Chronicle*, 16/3/1916.

The dates of the deaths make interesting reading and they give a clue as to the likely cause of most of them. Up until September 1918 there were only 12 fatalities at the camp, but after that the number rose steeply. There were 18 during the last quarter of 1918 and a further 15 in 1919. This dramatic increase coincided with the 1918 influenza pandemic, which eventually spread its deadly tendrils into the camp. There must have been some consternation in the camp at the rate the virus was spreading when, on 1 November 1918, the *Western Gazette* informed its readers that six prisoners had died of the effects of it during the previous weeks. Fortunately, although deaths continued right up until the eve of the prisoners' departure from Dorchester, one can imagine that things could have been much worse, and it is a testament to the medical staff and cleanliness of the camp that it was not.

After the War had ended, at the instigation of either the military or the local authorities, or the prisoners themselves, a memorial was created and placed in the vicinity of the graves to commemorate the men who had died in the camp. It was designed by one of the prisoners, K. Bartolmay, who also made some drawings of life within the camp. The memorial is a

Drawing done by prisoner Burtolmay in 1919 showing the memorial and graves of the dead prisoners. (Courtesy of the Dorset History Centre.)

tablet of Portland stone, upon which is carved, in relief, a kneeling German soldier holding a rifle. There are no names listed but it carries the words 'Hier Ruhen Deutsche Krieger in fremder erde doch unvergessen (Here lie German soldiers, in a foreign land but not forgotten). 1914 – Dorchester – 1919'.

For the period of the War the graves were tended by prisoners from the camp; post war the Imperial War Graves Commission, now known as the Commonwealth War Graves Commission, had responsibility for them. Locally, the Mill Street Mission[112] took over the actual tending of the graves and in November 1936 it got permission to plant shrubs and flowers on the graves.

It was also the Mill Street Mission that ensured that the dead prisoners would not be forgotten. On Armistice Day 1935 a wreath was placed at the memorial by the 5th Dorchester (Mill Street Mission) Scout Troop, and on 11 November 1938 the *Dundee Evening Telegraph* published the following article: 'Every year since 1918 a wreath has been laid by officials of the Mill Street Mission, Dorchester, on a German memorial at Fordington Cemetery,

A contingent of Dorchester boy scouts on parade at the German war memorial. (Copyright Mill Street Housing Society.)

112 The Mill Street Mission was started in 1905 in two thatched cottages at 57 Mill Street, Fordington, in what was the poorest and most insanitary part of Dorchester. The area had a reputation as a 'no-go' area and patrolling policemen were reputed to only enter the area in twos. Initially, the Mission had a hostile reception, but it persevered and became a much respected organisation (still operating today as the Mill Street Housing Society), adding much to the lives of the local residents. In 1929 the cottages were rebuilt and incorporated a purpose-built mission hall, which was within 100 m of the German memorial.

which lies amid graves of German soldiers who died while prisoners of War in Dorchester. Today the wreath was laid by a German woman, Sister Annie – Miss Annie Whistler – deaconess in charge of an organisation caring for orphans and homeless German children. She is the first German to have laid the wreath on this memorial on an Armistice Day. The wreath is inscribed "A token of praise and prayer for peace – Mill Street Mission". There were only five persons present at this ceremony, suggesting that the camp and its occupants had faded from the minds of the majority of Durnovarians.

In 1987, after rebuilding the Old Mill in Mill Street, the memorial window, commemorating both World Wars, from the original Mill Street Mission was incorporated. (Copyright Mill Street Housing Society.)

Sister Annie was not the only German to pay her respects at the memorial. In July 1936 a group of the Hitlerjugend,[113] led by Ernst Neudahl, arrived in the county town for a week's holiday. As well as attending the opening of the new nursing hospital

A group of Hitlerjugend pay their respects to their fallen comrades during their visit to Dorchester in 1936. (Copyright Mill Street Housing Society.)

113 Hitler Youth.

and witnessing the visit to Dorchester of the Lord Mayor of London, on the Sunday they visited the German graves at Fordington and placed a wreath bearing the words 'To the beloved memory of our fellow countrymen and gratitude for the respect and care of their resting place'. The party then sang a memorial hymn, planted bulbs and scattered soil brought from a Hamburg garden over the graves. Afterwards they went to the town's Cenotaph and placed a similar chapulet inscribed with the words 'To the memory of the men who fought that war should be no more. May they have not died in vain.' Then, having paid their respects to their countrymen the youths were taken to visit the Portland Naval Base at Weymouth by their hosts, the Dorchester Rotary Club, whose minute book records the enthusiasm of the young men for taking photographs inside the base.

A year later to the month, another group of Germans visited Dorchester. This time some of the former prisoners were paying a return visit, as guests of the British Legion. After a civic reception the party went to have tea with the mayor, Miss Winifred Marsden, who welcomed the 'comrades from Germany' and told them that she could well remember the days when some of them were in their midst only a short distance from the VAD hospital of 200 beds.[114] Some of their number had helped put up the hospital marquees and did other good work there. Then she referred to their 'magnificent band', which could be heard when the wind was blowing from the west. Finally, she hoped that the group would have a happy visit and 'take back to Germany pleasant memories of this dear old county town'.

The reply, made by Herr Spanuth, the leader of the group, was equally friendly but contained a message which, in hindsight, gives an inkling of some of the dark things that were happening in Germany at that time. He started by saying, 'We come here with the desire to lay our hands in yours in friendship,' and then added that it was 'A hard way and not always easy to follow, but it had to be done.' He then warned his English hosts that 'The culture of the western world is in danger' and 'that it is our belief that something needs to be done about it.' Herr Spanuth then begged his comrades from Germany to 'Stand and give three cheers for England. The England we love. The merry old England we saw yesterday.' The hosts were then saluted with a unified chorus of 'Heil, heil, heil'. One wonders what the folk of Dorchester made of the occasion. During their stay the Germans paid a visit to their old camp and left a wreath at the Fordington memorial adorned with a swastika, and another wreath was laid by the Mill Street

114 Winifred Marsden was Commandant of the Colliton VAD hospital in Dorchester and went on to become the first female mayor of Dorchester.

Two contrasting ceremonies at the German memorial. In the left image, on an earlier visit of the Hitler Youth in 1935, one member of the group salutes, Nazi style, the POWs who died in the camp. In the right photograph, taken 3 years later, a young German refugee places a wreath. (Copyright Mill Street Housing Society.)

Mission, bearing the words 'In remembrance of many happy friendships and the assurance of yet deeper desire for peace and goodwill with all.'[115]

An act of irony took place at the German memorial on Armistice Day 1939, when, as part of the service, a young girl stepped forward to lay a wreath. She was a refugee whose mother was a Jewish doctor.

Throughout the Second World War, the Mill Street Mission continued to arrange for wreaths to be laid at the memorial, despite the hostilities between the two countries. However, the messages that accompanied them tended to be more muted. The tribute in 1940, for example, which was laid by an Air Raid Warden, simply bore the words 'Memories and Hope.'[116]

As early as 1922 there was a proposal to move all the bodies of prisoners of war who had died in Britain to one central location. Negotiations began but became protracted and no agreement was reached. Perhaps memories of the War were just too raw in the negotiators' minds. However, in 1959 the British Government and the Federal Republic of Germany reached a consensus on the matter and in the early 1960s the remains of the dead prisoners buried in British soil were transferred to a communal cemetery on Cannock Chase in Staffordshire. There lie the bodies of most of the German prisoners of war who died in this country in both World Wars.

115 *Western Gazette*, 23/7/1937.
116 *Western Gazette*, 5/11/1940.

Cannock Chase German Military Cemetery, where the bodies of the German prisoners who died in Dorchester were finally laid to rest. The front left grave contains the remains of Johann Kaltenberger and Wilhelm Schmelzer.

Those prisoners who died in the Dorchester camp[117]

Name	Rank	Date died	Age
Bernhard Schneider	Soldat[118]	28/8/1915	25
Wilhelm Braun	Unteroffizier	6/12/1915	26
Emil Drygalla	Musketier[119]	10/3/1916	28
Alfred Hammel	Unknown	11/3/1916	19
Georg Meissner	Infanterist[120]	27/10/1916	34
Michail Reitinger	Infanterist	13/11/1916	31
Johannes Holste	Musketier	18/3/1917	20
Carl Becker	Musketier	7/4/1917	33
Adolf Mally	Musketier	25/4/1917	32
Johann Fischer	Grenadier[121]	14/6/1917	22
Hermann Woitkowski	Unteroffizier[122]	1/11/1917	31
Johann Kaltenberger	Krankentrager [123]	23/12/1917	41
Wilhelm Schmelzer	Seeman[124]	25/9/1918	29

117 List compiled from the burial records of Cannock Chase German Military Cemetery and those of Dorchester Borough.
118 Private.
119 Rifleman.
120 Infantryman.
121 As in the English word Grenadier, or grenade thrower.
122 Sergeant.
123 Stretcher bearer.
124 Sailor.

Name	Rank	Date died	Age
Hermann Hofmann	Soldat	17/10/1918	30
Karl Metzmacher	Musketier	26/10/1918	27
Paul Shotta	Unknown	27/10/1918	25
Edward Wannemacher	Gefreiter[125]	27/10/1918	29
Wilhelm Germann	Gefreiter	27/10/1918	32
Karl Grasedieck	Soldat	28/10/1918	34
Wilhelm Willms	Musketier	30/10/1918	20
Alfred Konrad	Gefreiter	2/11/1918	31
Karl Joos	Grenadier	2/11/1918	23
Hermann Rindefusse	Infanterist	4/11/1918	22
Lorenz Clauson	Unteroffizier	6/11/1918	28
Karl Heinz	Unknown	9/11/1918	28
Peter Kemmer	Infanterist	9/11/1918	37
Hugo Campe	Gefreiter	10/11/1918	37
Paul Nimmler	VizeFeldwebel[126]	11/11/1918	27
Emanual Prudlo	Gefreiter	23/11/1918	29
Alfred Borse	Unknown	24/11/1918	34
Joseph Kohler	Infanterist	1/1/1919	36
Ernst Zimmermann	Gefreiter	1/1/1919	27
Wilhelm Zimmermann	Gefreiter	7/2/1919	31
Martin Dingenthal	Soldat	28/2/1919	20
Heinrich Nollhoff	Unknown	15/3/1919	40
Victor Giera	Soldat	7/3/1919	29
Johann Schigulla	Musketier	18/3/1919	24
Peter Schauss	Unknown	18/3/1919	28
Paul Schwarz	Soldat	28/3/1919	22
Franz Radgowski	Musketier	17/5/1919	20
Frederick Kronenmeyer	Musketier	13/6/1919	20
Adalbert Betzoldt	Musketier	31/8/1919	22
Paul Boettcher	Gefreiter	23/10/1919	21
Jakob Oeffler	Gefreiter	25/10/1919	36
Robert Fischer	Musketier	29/10/1919	20

125 Corporal.
126 Senior NCO.

Article 18 of the Hague Convention stipulated that 'Prisoners of war shall enjoy complete liberty in the exercise of their religion; including the attendance at the services of whichever church they may belong to ....' In theory this right presented no problems, but the practice was more difficult. The vast majority of the prisoners in the camp who followed a religion were either Lutheran or Catholic and they needed somewhere to hold their services, and with potential congregations numbering hundreds this was no easy task.

Whilst Bruno Schmidt-Reder[127] was in the camp, during the first few months of its life, he observed that services were held in the open air by a Scottish protestant pastor, but with winter looming some type of indoor facility was required. We know from a contemporary photograph that one of the huts was used as a catholic chapel. It shows the altar, covered in a cloth bearing the motif of an Iron Cross, and an altarpiece, designed and built by the prisoners. Along one wall are what look like depictions of the Stations of the Cross. On a wooden plinth is a harmonium. For those of the protestant persuasion services were held in the Soldatenheim (Soldiers' Home).

The Stations of the Cross can be seen on the wall in this photograph of the Roman Catholic chapel. The altarpiece was carved by the prisoners. The man at the harmonium looks very precarious on the plinth. (Courtesy of the Keep Military Museum.)

127 See page 42.

The catholic looks to his priest and the Lutheran to his pastor for spiritual guidance, but it appears that neither were present among the prisoners for long periods of the camp's life. This was certainly the case in the early period of the war and, consequently, it fell to the Dorchester clergy to officiate at the camp, as well as performing other religious duties, such as funerals. The *Western Gazette* informed its readers that 'On Sunday 23 August 1914 the Rev. Father Shepherd said Mass for the Catholic prisoners, numbering about a hundred, including some naval officers. His ministrations will continue regularly. The Rev. R.S. Holmes, Congregational Minister, will also take part in caring for the spiritual welfare of prisoners of the Protestant faith.'[128]

An article in the *Western Gazette* dated 18 September 1914 reported: 'On Sunday morning Father Shepherd said mass to about 200 Catholics and in the afternoon the Rev. R.S. Holmes conducted the usual service for the Lutherans. The band of the prisoners of war again helped in the service. The London branch of the YMCA for Germans have kindly promised to send a supply of hymn sheets. In response to an appeal from the Rev. R.S. Holmes, Congregational minister, who has undertaken the spiritual care of the Lutherans, among the thousand odd prisoners of war under Col Block's charge at the artillery barracks, the British and Foreign Bible Society have sent him 150 copies of the New Testament in German; and an equal number of German gospels. Col Capel Brunker[129] has also sent a large parcel of German gospels to Canon Cohard, acting chaplain to the garrison, who has passed them on to Mr Holmes for distribution. The grant of bibles was especially fortunate, as owing to these books being printed in Berlin, there is now but a very limited supply available in England. Mr Michael Morrison, who has for 38 years been agent to the Bible Society in Germany, is now in England, and, having got leave to visit the prisoners for spiritual discourse, came to Dorchester on Saturday afternoon and went to the camp in company with Mr Holmes. He left Dorchester again the same evening.'

More religious books followed soon after; 150 German New Testaments arrived from the British and Foreign Bible Society, plus 300 hymn sheets, containing 17 hymns from the German YMCA in London. It was not long before the hymn sheets were put to good use. Soon a prison choir was formed,

128 *Western Gazette*, 28/8/1914.

129 Capel Molyneux Brunker DSO CMG (1858-1936). Professional soldier who competed for Britain in the horse jumping event at the 1924 Olympic Games.

which rehearsed with a band of seven musicians.[130] A further consignment brought the number of New Testaments up to 550.

Rev Holmes was the Pastor of Dorchester's Congregational church and became very popular with the prisoners, as was demonstrated in November 1914. At the close of one of his Sunday services, which he held every week, he was presented with a large silver inkstand, a pair of silver candlesticks and an illuminated address, which was signed by the 100 contributors. The silver plate was engraved and the inkstand bore the words 'Zur Erinerung an die Deutsche Kriegs-Gefangenen, Dorchester 1914'.[131] The candlesticks were etched with the pastor's initials and the text of the illuminated address read 'Gewidmet von Kriegs-Gefangenen das Lagers, Dorchester, Ihren Werten Herra Pastor Holmes 1914'.[132] On hearing of the presentation, Mr Matthew H. Tilley, the veteran Dorset apiarist, sent 40 lb of Dorset honey for the enjoyment of the donors.

In March 1917, a Pastor Scholten from London was conducting services regularly at the camp, and there were occasions when German officers and officials conducted prisoner funerals. Religious festivals like Easter and Christmas were particularly important times for Catholics and Protestants alike. Over the 3 days of the Christmas period of 1916 a total of eight services were held, two of which were conducted by the aforementioned Pastor Scholten and another two by Herr Gauntlett, also from London. The camp also had its own branch of the YMCA which was busy with organising Christmas celebrations.[133]

---

130 *Western Gazette*, 25/9/1914.

131 'In memory of the German prisoners of war, Dorchester, 1914.'

132 'Dedicated by the prisoners of war of the camp, Dorchester, to their honoured Pastor Holmes, 1914.'

133 *Deutsche Blätter*.

Work

Article 6 of the Hague Convention relating to the treatment of prisoners of war stated that capturing states could use the labour of prisoners, according to their rank and aptitude. The tasks were not to be excessive and were to have no connection with the operations of the war. Prisoners could be authorised to do public service, work for private persons or work on their own account, and their rate of pay for such work was to be agreed with the military authorities. The wages of the prisoners were to go towards improving their position, and the balance was to be paid them on their release, after deducting the cost of their maintenance. Officers and senior NCOs were not required to work.

Despite this very clear mandate regarding the employment of prisoners of war incarcerated in the UK, it was not until 1916 that the British Government came up with an official scheme. Several reasons were given for this reluctance. When questions were asked as to why, when so many men were leaving their jobs to join the army, a readily available workforce of prisoners of war was not being used, one of the reasons given was that the public did not want to see jobs that had been filled by British men being done by the enemy. Another was that employers in the private sector did not want the responsibility of managing groups of workers, many of whom could not speak English and might prove troublesome. The trade unions feared that the pay and conditions of indigenous workers might be undermined by POW labour.

Lord Newton, Under Secretary of State for Foreign Affairs, showed his frustration with the situation in the House of Lords, declaring, 'I am quite prepared to confess that in my opinion the situation generally as regards the employment of prisoners is by no means satisfactory, and I agree with my noble friend that it would be difficult to conceive a more ludicrous spectacle than that which is afforded to us at the present moment. Here we are, with an alarming scarcity of labour throughout the country, imploring women to come to our assistance, whilst there are thousands of able-bodied prisoners in this country who are doing very little work at all.'[134] He went on to say that he understood that the Government had been told that the railway owners and dockers would have nothing to do with them and the miners would not speak to them.

134 House of Lords Parliamentary Debates.

It appears that the military and civil authorities in Dorset had no such reservations, even though the local trade unions put a block on prisoners building their own huts because it took work away from local firms. The outbreak of war could not have come at a worse time for a farming county like Dorset. The harvest was waiting to be brought in and at the same time patriotic carters and farm labours were responding to Lord Kitchener's call to join the New Army. So, it was not long before some of the Dorchester prisoners were working on local farms. Evidence of this is contained in a postcard dated 7 September 1914, written by a Dorchester resident to a friend, in which she says, 'The Germans go out harvesting where wanted and they went to one place and after they worked till 4.30 the farmer refused to give them anything to eat. They were not very pleased about it and now they won't go out.' The lady also mentioned that she had heard the German band giving a concert in the Barracks.

Nor was it long before the County Council became aware of what it saw as a free workforce on its doorstep. At their meeting in November 1914, they were told by the Chairman of the Works Committee that it could not recommend a programme of works because of the shortage of labour and suggested that they ask the government to consider the use of the Dorchester internees. Although the outcome of the request was pending, the Chairman understood that the Government was aware that continuous confinement could lead to unrest and that some kind of work would be a good thing. The latter comment brought cries of 'Hear, Hear' from the council members.[135]

Dorchester Town Council also took advantage of prisoner labour. In February 1916, it applied to the military authorities for permission to allow Germans to work in the Borough Gardens. The precedent had already been established, as prisoners were already being employed at the town's sewage works and in local timber yards, and consequently the application was granted.[136] The work of the foreign gardeners, which included maintaining lawns and flower beds and lopping trees and shrubs, did not go unnoticed. At a meeting of the Town Council on 9 October 1917, Councillor John Walne introduced some levity into the debate when he asked Joseph Porter, Chairman of the Recreation and Amusement Committee, whether it was with his sanction or approval that the prisoners at work in the Borough Gardens had designed one of the decorative flower beds in the shape of a German Iron Cross. He added that it had been cut that morning and wondered whether the Germans had done it out of devilment. Far from

135 *Western Gazette*, 6/11/1916.
136 *Newcastle Daily Journal*, 26/2/1916.

treating it as a serious business there were peals of laughter from the council members, especially when Councillor Higgins suggested that it appeared that the Germans were doing a little gardening of their own. At the request of the Council the Chairman of the Committee and Mr Harman Strange, the Borough Surveyor, later visited the Borough Gardens with a reporter from the *Chronicle* in tow, to inspect the offending flower bed. The display did, indeed, look suspiciously like the shape of an Iron Cross, so they decided to interview the head gardener, Mr Harris, who assured them that the bed had been the same shape, a Maltese Cross, for the last 15 years and that it was originally laid out by his father.[137]

The efforts of the prisoners came to the attention of the Council again, in February 1918, when one of the councillors, Dr Elias Kerr, said that there had been shocking mutilation going on in the Borough Gardens and instead of being a place of beauty, the Gardens looked more like a hen house. Councillor Miles replied that the German prisoners had done all the labour, and the shrubs, etc. were all the better for seeing a little daylight. Dr Kerr had occasion to display his displeasure again at the following month's council meeting, when the committee were told that the gardens were now in very good shape. Thanks to the work of the Germans the park looked less like a wood, now that new flower beds had been established. The majority agreed, but Kerr said that he deplored what had been done. At the same meeting the cost of maintaining the Gardens was queried, because annual expenditure had risen from £150 for 1917 to £176 for 1918. It was explained that the main reason for the rise was an increase in the wages of the prisoners, as ordered by the War Office. The prisoners employed as gardeners did not confine their enthusiastic pruning skills to the Borough Gardens. Several of the splendid Lime trees planted around the town, including those at the Junction, were pollarded by them and continued to be cut in the same manner for several decades afterwards. POWs were also used to sweep the streets of Dorchester.

Demand for prisoner labour was not confined to public service. For instance, Mr Rolfe Pope, eldest son of the brewer Alfred, lived in Culliford House in Icen Way, which had a large kitchen garden tended by a working party of men from the camp. Their German foreman liked to eat his midday meal with a knife and fork and after his repast always took his utensils to Mrs Guppy, the cook of the house, to be washed.[138]

With such a large number of prisoners in the camp there was bound to

137 Samuel Harris ran a nursery on the site of the Gardens before selling it to the Town Council in 1895 for use as public gardens.

138 Story told to me by a member of the Pope family.

Prisoners of war sweeping High East Street. (Courtesy of Dorset County Museum.)

be a great array of skills available. Cabinet-maker Louis Voss employed five prisoners in his cabinet-making business at 14 Princes Street, overseen by two guards, and working parties were sent to Eddison's Steam Plough Works and Channons, motor engineers, where, in the latter case, they machined shells and fuses for the Army, work that clearly contravened the Hague Convention.[139]

There are still people in Dorchester who remember when, as children, their parents had occasion to visit the shop of James Miles, the saddler, at 14 High West Street. Inside the shop was a life-sized model of a dappled grey horse, onto which the excited child was put. But, the horse wasn't always grey. When the saddler acquired it the horse was a bay, but he did not like the colour, so he employed a prisoner to repaint it.

There were, of course, any amount of jobs to be done inside the camp, which kept some of the prisoners occupied but by no means all. When Van der Veer and his fellow correspondents visited the camp at the end of

139 Skyrme.

James Miles' horse repainted by a German prisoner. (Source: P. Lacey.)

1915 he reported that, except for cleaning their rooms, there was no compulsory work for the prisoners. A Scandinavian reporter, present at the time, was heard to remark to a representative of a leading New York newspaper, 'I think I will enlist in the German Army in order to be made a POW in Dorchester. I should have a splendid time, no work, good food and every convenience.'[140] Van der Veer noted that those prisoners that were working were employed in the day to-day running of the camp and were well paid. Clothing and boots were repaired in tailors' and cobblers' workshops, while other trades recorded included printing, hairdressing, bookbinding and carpentry. The men, who were employed either as day labourers or as craftsmen, were earning up to 6 shillings per week in January 1916. If an article that was printed in the *Western Times* is to be believed it appears that the boot repairers were kept very busy, mending boots from other places. In March 1919, a German prisoner was up before the magistrates for stealing some leather to repair his boots. A Sergeant explained to the court that two lots of boots needing repair had been sent to the camp at Dorchester the previous November and January, but none of them had yet been returned.[141]

Even with all the day-to-day jobs required to keep the camp running smoothly, the majority of the prisoners had time on their hands, plus there were those who were not fit enough to do manual work on farms or elsewhere. To alleviate this problem, outside work was brought into the camp. Making mailbags became the principal occupation, at a wage of 6 d per bag, and, according to the Swiss legation that visited in March 1917, 65,000 had been made, but production had since ceased. Agricultural thermometers were also being produced at a rate of 300 per week. The money that the men earned resulted in the development of an internal economy and an

140 *Manchester Evening News*, 18/12/1915.
141 *Western Times*, 11/3/1919.

Items like this picture frame, made in the camp's carpentry workshop, were exchanged as part of the camp's internal economy. (Source: Item in the ownership of D. Pride.)

extensive bartering system, where cigars were exchanged for foodstuffs and peaked caps for rabbits. Prisoners also bought and sold items, such as things made in the carpenters' workshop, so that they could purchase items from the canteen. In December 1916 the exchange rate was 10 English pence for 1 German Mark.[142]

Despite initial opposition by local trade unionists to the use of prisoner labour to extend the camp, in March 1917 over 200 men were busy in the carpenters' workshop producing sections for new huts. In addition, prisoners were used for road building within the camp, and it was whilst this was going on that some prisoners, reportedly, dug up some bones which were claimed to be those of French prisoners of war who had been detained in the barracks during the Napoleonic Wars. However, the only evidence for this is an article in an American newspaper[143] and there are no local references to it. The same article informed its readers that some of the prisoners were being paid 2 d an hour for digging drainage ditches to alleviate the muddy condition of the unpaved walkways, caused by recent heavy rain.

One discovery that did make the local headlines was when a party of men working on Poundbury hill fort unearthed a lead coffin and two big stone ones. Evidently, it took six men to lift the lid off one of the caskets, which was found to contain a small skeleton. Thomas Hardy, the author, who was attending a meeting of antiquarians in Dorchester at the time, said that the discovery bore out the tradition that Poundbury was a Saxon burial ground.

The catalysts that brought about the introduction of a formal Government scheme for using POWS in agriculture came not from this country but from the battlefields abroad and the activities of German U-boats. Due to heavy losses on the Western Front the British Government passed the Military Service Act in January 1916, which brought in conscription. Now, single men between the ages of 18 and 41 could be called up for military service,

142 *Deutsche Blätter.*
143 *Reading Eagle,* 7/1/1916.

and in the following May the liability was extended to married men. This meant that the rate at which agricultural workers left the land increased, the effects of which were demonstrated by the number of requests to Military Service Tribunals by farmers and landowners seeking exemption for their workers because they could not cope without them.[144]

In May 1916, Mr Scutt, a farmer from Watercombe, appeared before the Dorchester Rural Military Service Tribunal, seeking exemption from military service for his employee Walter Masters, on the grounds that his permanent workforce had already been depleted severely. He informed the tribunal that he had ten Germans on his farm at Maiden Castle, just outside Dorchester, but that he could not get them out as far as Watercombe, which was 7 miles away. In reply to a question from Canon Hankey, a member of the tribunal, he said that the prisoners worked from nine in the morning until half past four and that they worked very well.[145]

The need to maximise home food production was heightened by the effects of unrestricted attacks by German submarines on merchant ships, which were bringing food into the UK, mainly from Canada and the USA, and by 1916 the situation was becoming critical. Now farmers were urged to bring every spare acre of land into production and the Government, on its part, at last devised a scheme to increase the use of prisoner labour on the land.

War Agricultural Committees were set up in the counties to liaise with farmers, and in November 1916, the Dorset Committee were introduced to the Government's scheme in a letter from Maj. Gen. Schlater,[146] commanding officer of Southern Military Command. They were asked to give particulars of any farmers in the county who wanted prisoners of war, stating the number of men required, details of what separate accommodation was available for the prisoners and their guards, the nature of the work and the qualifications required for the various jobs. On its part, the War Office said that only men of good character would be sent to employers, together with an interpreter, that the rate of pay was to be the same as the current rates for similarly skilled British employees, and that arrangements for the feeding of prisoners and their guards would be made by the military authorities. It was also stated

144 Military Service Tribunals were set up to hear appeals from men who had been notified that they were required to enlist. Legitimate reasons for exemption included working in a reserved occupation, family hardship or conscientious objection. Employers could also appeal against an employee being enlisted, on the grounds that their business would be affected detrimentally by the employee's absence.

145 *Western Gazette*, 26/5/1916.

146 Maj. Gen. (later General) Sir Henry Schlater, Commander, Southern Command UK, 1916–1919.

that parties of prisoners numbering less than five were undesirable and groups between 20 and 25 were more suitable.[147]

This scheme might have worked, but the Government amended it and made it very difficult to implement. The problems were highlighted at a meeting of the Dorset War Agricultural Committee (DWAC) in January 1917. The Chairman said that the scheme appeared to be very complex and puzzling because, although the Government promised that a certain number of prisoners could be made available, there were so many conditions and regulations attached to the process that, except in a few isolated cases, it was impossible to use them. Seventy-five prisoners from Dorchester had been reserved to work in the county, but housing had to be found for them and for the guard of 35. In addition, the prisoners could only be employed within 5 miles of their place of accommodation, unless the farmer was prepared to provide transport. Pay was to be as for local labour, with two rates, one for skilled men and another for unskilled. All in all, the Committee were not impressed with the scheme and felt that the time taken out of the day collecting and returning prisoners, plus having to ensure that they stopped for a midday meal, hardly made it worthwhile.

Despite the problems, the Committee began to look around for suitable places to house the workers. In January 1917, the Sherborne Guardians of the Poor were considering whether or not prisoners from Dorchester should be housed in the local workhouse. The Master said that he could rearrange things so that the local inmates were not inconvenienced, but some of the prisoners might have to sleep on the floors. The Committee decided to reconsider the situation when the next military tribunal had decided whether or not the Master of the workhouse was exempt from military service.

There were other local barriers to employing prisoners. In July 1917, the DWAC received representations about the excessive charge made for the hire of POWs. Mr Jesty, a local farmer, said that when the Germans first started to work, the rate was 1½ d per hour but it had since risen to 4 d, and that was when he stopped employing them. Mr Ismay added that the German cook who accompanied the workers to their place of work had also to be paid for doing nothing productive. There was also the question of security. Much of the southern part of Dorset was out of bounds for the employment of prisoners because they were not allowed to work within 10 miles of the sea. One person affected by this regulation was Mrs Debenham, whose family farmed in a restricted area. Then, of course, there were those people who

147 *Western Gazette*, 24/11/1916.

were simply not prepared to use POW labour because they were the enemy. An example of this arose in May 1918, at a rally held in Sherborne to raise recruits for the Women's Land Army. The large audience listening to the speeches were very enthusiastic, but their enthusiasm reached a crescendo when one of the speakers declared that no German would ever come on his soil. This opinion was in marked contrast to another person at the meeting who asked why women were being required to work on the land when there were so many prisoners of war available.[148]

It became clear to the authorities that if any scheme for employing prisoner labour was to work they would have to provide centres of accommodation, and this they did. The DWAC in July 1918 were informed that the Food Production Department had come up with a scheme for using migratory gangs of POW labour that would work from a central depot, where they would be housed, going out to local farms, as required. However, the Committee felt that in view of the fact that the harvest was just weeks away, there was not enough time to make the necessary arrangements. But, just a month later they appear to have changed their minds and were discussing how prisoners who were skilled ploughmen could be used in those areas of the county that were more suitable for cultivation by the horse than the tractor. It was decided that they would be housed in centres at Beaminster, Marshwood, Sturminster Newton and Almer. Horses would be supplied and rationed by the Government, and farmers were to be charged 20–35 shillings an acre for the work.

Eventually, additional agricultural depots were established at other places, including Bradford Abbas, Gillingham and Spetisbury, and a number of other types of work camp sprung up at Blandford, Bovington, Iwerne Minster, Long Crichel, Swanage, Wareham, Wimborne, Wool and Louds Mill in Dorchester. These were for all manner of employment. At one of the two camps at Blandford, for instance, prisoners were employed in tree felling and working in a saw mill, whilst from the camp at Sturminster Newton the men went to work in a quarry. As noted elsewhere, Dorchester had a large number of camps and depots under its jurisdiction located outside Dorset. Members of the Swiss legation, visiting the Dorchester camp on 28 March 1919, were told that nationally the number of work camps affiliated to Dorchester was 130 (see Appendix 3), and that, of the prisoners working outside the Dorchester camp, 507 were employed in Royal Engineers' workshops, 40 by the Royal Engineers in Dorchester Town, 200 in railway

148 *Western Gazette*, 7/6/1918.

construction and 318 made up outside working parties on agricultural and other work.

Inevitably, the additional number of prisoners working out in the countryside led to more problems. In August 1918 the Prisoners of War Department visited some of the places of work and discovered that many of the German gang leaders were not working in the fields with their charges. It also found that many of the prisoners were not employed fully. Some of the farmers complained that prisoners were being sent from the camps with insufficient food, and that they begged for more, saying that they could not be expected to work unless they were sufficiently fed. It was stated that in some cases the prisoners only had a handful of oatmeal and a few potatoes for a day's work, and that in other cases their midday meal consisted of a herring that was on the wrong side of fresh. On the other hand, someone else suggested that rations were ample, but that the prisoners preferred to leave most of it back at the depot, relying on the generosity of the farmer for their repast. A further complaint was that the guards were inattentive. In one case a guard was found sitting in the town while the prisoners were at work on top of a hill.

A curious case of irony arose in Dorset, when one group of German prisoners refused to work with British conscientious objectors. On the other hand, others felt that there was a definite benefit of the two groups working together. A young tenant farmer named Hobbs appeared before the Dorchester Rural Military Tribunal in March 1917, seeking exemption from military service because he was a conscientious objector, although he was willing to work at home and said that he had been offered employment on the farm of Mr William Cann, at Southover, Frampton, who had ten Germans working on the land, hoeing roots. The tribunal agreed that Hobbs could remain at home working on the farm, but the Chairman could not help adding his own comment that working with German prisoners would hopefully improve the attitude of the conscientious objector.[149]

Prisoners were not confined to working on conventional farms. One material that was essential for the war effort was flax. It was used for webbing, belts and straps, and as the War developed it was needed increasingly to make the linen that covered the wings of aircraft. Locally, the centre for the growing of flax was just over the Dorset border around the town of Yeovil in Somerset. In June 1918, 3,460 acres of the crop were waiting to be harvested, a long laborious process that could only be done by hand. The labour force of

149 *Western Gazette*, 9/3/1917.

between 2,000 and 3,000 required to do this job included 300 prisoners sent from Dorchester, and in this instance the rule of Germans not working with women was ignored. The prisoners must have thought that they had died and gone to heaven because most of the remainder of the workforce was female. Some were college students, others volunteers, known as City Workers, and another contingent were described as 'Scotch university lasses'.[150]

The coast between Charmouth and Lyme Regis is very unstable and in 1916 there was a landslide, making the adjacent road dangerous, to the extent that a new one was required. The intention was to build a new highway, 2½ miles long, using mainly POW labour, and arrangements were made with the military authorities for a maximum of 200 to be employed. The rate of pay was to be commensurate with that of unskilled labour in the area, 'bearing in mind the fact that prisoners could not be expected to give such satisfactory service as ordinary civilian labour'.[151] A hundred of the men were to work in quarries for 3 months, digging out enough material to construct 6,000 yards of road, at a rate of pay of 1 s 6 d per yard. A further 50 were to be employed lowering gradients to the road and another 50 removing undergrowth and topsoil, and operating a temporary tramway. But, the Council must have had other priorities and missed the opportunity, because in November 1919, while they were still debating about what to do, their captive workforce returned to their native land.

Clearly, the use of POW labour during the War was fraught with problems, particularly in the area of agriculture, where it was most needed. Whilst organisations, both national and local, existed for implementing a scheme to help agricultural counties like Dorset, it was the practical difficulties on the ground that mitigated against success. Housing, guarding, feeding and transporting of prisoners were all problematical. On the farms it was women who did the lion's share. In December 1918 the number of prisoners working on farms, nationally, was at its height, at 30,000, compared to around 250,000 women who worked in agriculture during the War, plus a large number of children, such as Boy Scouts and Girl Guides. In other areas of work the employment of prisoners was more successful. These were jobs like quarrying and tree felling, which required heavy labour and were not considered to be jobs that women could do. In Dorchester, the employment of prisoner labour provided an opportunity for the local population to come into contact with the enemy and to understand that they too were human beings.

150 *Western Gazette*, 28/6/1918.
151 *Western Gazette*, 4/8/1916.

Recreation

The first weeks of incarceration were a surreal experience for a prisoner. On the one hand, he had time to think and remember his life before being captured, and, on the other, he was trying to come to terms with his new situation. Everything was new and there was much to learn: the rules of the camp, which were read out by the commandant on arrival, getting used to sharing a hut with strangers, and becoming accustomed to camp routine. But, at some stage, the new and the novel were replaced by the same old and the monotonous, and the prisoner was faced with the realities of imprisonment. These included separation from his family for an indefinite period, an all-male environment, basic food and accommodation, and endless hours that needed to be filled, all of which could have serious effects on his mental and physical health.

This drawing by K. Bartolmay, who designed the German war memorial, is entitled Dreaming and reflects the feeling of isolation felt by many of the prisoners. (Courtesy of the Keep Military Museum)

The situation was aptly described by a writer in the *Deutsche Blätter*, when he wrote: 'After the battlefield, exhaustion sets in. The prisoner only thinks of sleep and peace and escapes into memories of a happier existence pre-war … the first kiss, the first exam, walking and their dreams of the future at that time, hot summer nights, anything to blot out the present time. The longer the imprisonment, the heavier the heart became and spirits began to flag. Little by little the ability to escape to the past in search of happier thoughts became more difficult. An irritability, a constant feeling of unrest, a deep joylessness, and general discord manifested itself in the form of "prison crazy" and "campitis".'[152]

The problem of boredom was

152 John Yarnall examines this phenomenon in his book.

highlighted also by one of Dorchester's civilian internees. In a letter to a New York friend, dated 29 October 1914, Capt. Tarnow, the commander of the Hamburg-America Line steamer *Prinz Joachim*, told his correspondent that 'The worst is, time hangs so heavily on my hands. I often hardly know how to pass my day. I cannot even write letters, as only two are allowed to be written per week and they must not be longer than two pages each. There is nothing left but Mark Twain's advice: "Smoke up".'[153]

Throughout the life of the camp, a wide variety of clubs and diversions sprung up to keep the men occupied. As early as November 1914 the prisoners, with the aid of the Camp Commandant, had formed recreational facilities, which included a school and a lecture room. The school was set up in the old hardball court of the artillery barracks, where the area was roofed over and a conventional schoolmaster's desk placed on a platform above rows of benches, which were occupied by classes studying an extensive curriculum. One of the German tutors of English was reported to be a young judge from the city of Münster in North Rhine-Westphalia, and Van der Veer noted on his visit to the camp that a young German was teaching Egyptian history. By June 1915 courses were being offered in subjects such as accountancy, English, French, geography and history, split into beginners and advanced classes, often aided by photographs.

Students enjoying an English class. (Courtesy of the Keep Military Museum.)

Very popular at that time was the farming course which had 125 participants, but it was not without its difficulties, because the teachers came and went and it became an on-going struggle to maintain a high standard.[154] For those interested in horticulture there was an extensive garden, dotted here and there with wooden benches and gazebos made in the camp, and rabbits were

153 *New York Times*, 3/12/1914.
154 *Deutsche Blätter.*

The prisoners had a large garden, where they grew flowers and vegetables. (Courtesy of the Keep Military Museum.)

This photograph is in stark contrast to some of the propaganda images showing the Germans as devils. (Courtesy of the Keep Military Museum.)

kept in hutches built in the void under the elevated huts. The Government film depicting life in the camp shows the men handling their pets with great affection and some are on leads. There is no evidence that the rabbits were used as food, but, with so many of the prisoners coming from communities where rabbits were normally bred for that purpose, it is quite likely that some ended up in the pot. In any event, it appears that by July 1918 the camp was rabbit free, if one of the prison guards, a Sgt Maj. Trineman, was to be believed. When, as a witness in the trial of the baker Thomas Greenwood, he was asked about rabbits being kept, he declared, 'There are no rabbits in my camp.'[155]

The prisoners liked to keep rabbits. Note the hutches built under the hut. (Courtesy of the Keep Military Museum.)

One important facility, opened on 4 July 1916, told everyone, in big letters printed over the door, that it was the 'Soldatenheim' (Soldiers' Home). This

155 See page 52.

large wooden building, which was donated by the American YMCA and bore the organisation's logo, gave the prisoner a chance to escape from the general noise of the camp, providing he could pay the 1 Pfennig monthly subscription to those fellow prisoners who ran the facility. Here he could study, with the aid of 900 reference books, read English newspapers, which were censored, magazines or general literature. Newspapers from enemy countries were not allowed. One woman, a Miss Smith-Marriot of Down House, Blandford, added to the camp's library when she donated a parcel of mostly German books, and in November 1917 Thomas Hardy, after a visit to the camp, arranged for the prisoners to receive translations of his works. Another source of reading material was the publishing company Deutsche Dichter Gedächtnis Stiftung, which provided 10,682 books to prisoners of war in Britain between August 1914 and December 1917.

The Soldatenheim (Soldiers' Home) drawn by prisoner H. Delfs. The hut was provided by the YMCA, whose motif of a triangle can be seen. (Courtesy of the Keep Military Museum.)

Reading was not the only recreation that went on in the Soldatenheim: a photograph shows prisoners playing draughts and chess, in a well-lit room. The chess club was one of many clubs, and in December 1916 it was meeting on Tuesday, Wednesday and Sunday evenings for three and a half hours, and should a chess player be unfortunate enough to lose one of his game pieces all was not lost. He had merely to pop along to Row 6, Hut 5, where he would find the home of the wood-turning club, which could make a new one. This little enterprise advertised itself in the camp newspaper, offering to make whistles, smoking pipes, tobacco tampers and violin bows, as well as chess pieces. As one can imagine, the camp contained some very skilled persons.

Catching up with the news. (Courtesy of the Keep Military Museum.)

Some of the prisoners produced intricately carved wooden objects, some of which were given to the guards.[156]

Like many prison camps, home and abroad, Dorchester produced its own newspaper. The lifespan of the *Deutsche Blätter des Kriegsgefangenenlagers*

Enjoying a game of draughts in the Soldatenheim. (Courtesy of the Keep Military Museum.)

156 See photograph on page 127.

This photograph is entitled 'Receiving the newspapers'. Note the rain-water conduits in the roadway. The function of the footbridge in the distance is unknown. (Courtesy of the Keep Military Museum.)

Dorchester, to give it its full title, is unknown and only one copy, published in December, 1916, appears to have survived. The newspaper could be posted home and, because of this, the proofs had to be scrutinised by the censor before they were sent to be printed outside. Crosswords, puzzles and chess problems were not allowed in case they contained covert messages. The copy that survives is dated 24 December and makes interesting reading. The four-page broadsheet has an editorial which discusses whether prisoners of war should receive the same rate of pay as their fighting comrades, for the period of their captivity. It contains an article on the history of Dorchester from Roman times. Articles also talk about the plight of the prisoner and the daily routine. Perhaps because it is coming to the end of the year, much of the remainder looks back at the development of sporting and social activities in the camp, and a whole page is devoted to notices relating to times of religious services, sporting fixtures and social events.

Music and theatre played a large part in the social life in POW camps and Dorchester was no exception, where performances were produced to a high standard. The first reference to music occurs very early on in the first few weeks of the camp's life, when the *Chronicle* reported in August 1914 that a number of military reservists arrived, carrying sufficient instruments to form a creditable wind and string band.[157] The problem, of course, was that these early musicians were civilian internees and it was not long before they were moved on to other camps, taking their instruments with them. Those that replaced them came straight from the battlefields, or were saved from sinking ships and submarines, so were most unlikely to be carrying anything more musical than a harmonica.

157 *Chronicle*, 20/8/1914.

Despite this, music in the camp did not die, thanks to the determination of some of the prisoners. Table knives were honed into crude woodworking tools and used to carve wooden planks, and later, as conventional tools became available, carpenters put their skills to use and produced violins and a cello, and, with the addition of a piano brought in from outside, the first string trio was formed. From these humble beginnings things went from strength to strength. After negotiations with the Camp Commandant, brass instruments were acquired, although for a period they were taken away, possibly as a punishment for the escapes of 1915.

At the end of 1915 the venue for concerts and recitals was transferred from the gymnasium, which was deemed to be too small, to the new theatre building. As instruments were added, the orchestra grew and performed a wide variety of music and opera under its director and conductor Herr Geisenhoner. As well as the large orchestra, there was a theatre band and a very popular singing group named 'Germania', directed by Herr Petrusch. At the end of the War each member of the choir was presented with a scroll, upon which was written 'To the memory of the beautiful hours spent singing German songs whilst in English captivity'.[158] Another style of music was provided by a group of mandolin players called 'Edelweiss'.

A few concert programmes have survived[159] and they give some idea of the variety of music that was performed in the camp. On 9 October 1918, the large orchestra, conducted by Kurt Adler, played pieces by Mozart, Weber and Schubert, plus a number of operatic excerpts from Don Juan, sung by Adolf Zipf. On a lighter note, a programme of popular classical pieces, which included waltzes and marches, was held in June 1919, and on one occasion the music club got together with the gymnastics club to present a mixed programme of music and gymnastics. The performance opened with Johann Strauss's

The camp band performing on the parade ground. (Courtesy of the Keep Military Museum.)

158 BA/MA/200/1878.
159 BA/MSG200/1957.

overture from Die Fledermaus, followed by displays of floor exercises, vaulting and work on the parallel bars. Music was not confined to the theatre hall. The *Deutsche Blätter* informed its readers that 'Music abounds in the camp; it is to be found in every room, every barrack', adding that 'Bad people do not have songs'.

The theatre club was kept very busy producing plays, reviews and vaudeville performances, and while there was no shortage of people willing to help, scenery had to be built and costumes made or bought in. In December 1915 a purpose-built theatre was constructed, and in August 1918 the club celebrated its 200th performance with a production of 'Jugenfreunde' by Ludwig Fulda, with prisoners Meissler and Klockow taking the female parts. During 1918 and 1919 one play was staged about every 2 weeks and at the close of the camp nearly 300 productions had been put on. The theatre club took its job very seriously: 'Things were not without worry. What worries one might ask, sneeringly? Why everything you see before you – the stage, the set, curtains, expensive wigs, corsets petticoats, make-up, costumes, from the beautiful evening dresses to the night gown of a professor has to be found, bought or made. Everything has to be covered by the cost of the entrance fee. You want to see the real thing (even men playing the part of the "little woman" must come across as true portrayals) not scarecrows. The German theatre is glad to fight for it all and will continue to do so.'[160]

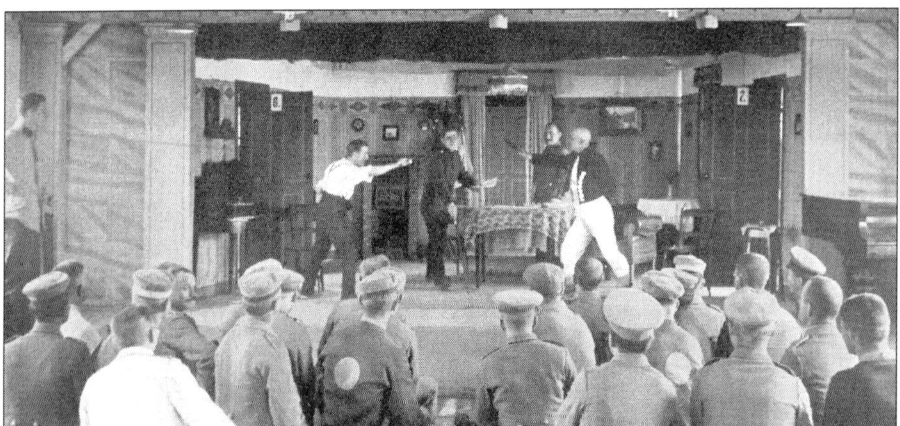

Prisoners enjoy one of the many plays put on in the camp theatre. Two prisoners have a yellow identity disk on the back of their tunics.[161] *(Courtesy of the Keep Military Museum.)*

160 *Deutsche Blätter.*

161 When prisoners were issued with civilian clothes, because their uniforms were unserviceable, tunics and jackets were adorned with a large yellow circle, so that if they escaped they were easily recognised.

One interesting item surviving from the camp is a hand-written draft programme for the 'Grand Review Cirkus Sarrasini', performed by the Prisoner Troupe. Ringmaster Stollberg urged patrons to get to their seats at least half an hour before the start of the performance as the demand for tickets was bound to be great. Acts included August and Tinnes, the comedy duo; also the 'best acrobat in the world', and finished with the playing of the William Tell Overture by the theatre band.[162]

If hobby clubs and lessons looked after cerebral health, it was sport that contributed to the prisoners' physical well-being. The *Deutsche Blätter* recalled that during its early life prisoners were confined to walking around the camp for exercise, although a photograph does show a group of men playing handball on the old parade ground of the artillery barracks, before it was covered with huts. The answer was to establish a purpose-built sports field, by fencing off part of the hill fort to the north of the camp. A running track, football pitch and hockey pitches were marked out and a sandpit built for jumping, and it was not long before sports groups began to mushroom, including those for athletics, hockey, football and rounders. Nor was exercise confined to the outdoors; in the gymnasium a prisoner could take part in gymnastics, bodybuilding, weightlifting, wrestling and fistball. The camp newspaper commented

This photograph, taken early on in the life of the camp, shows prisoners playing on the parade ground of the artillery barracks.

The sports ground, a popular place to exercise or just meet friends. (Courtesy of the ICRC.)

162 BA/MA/200/1878.

that 'Interest grew amazingly fast. The sports area had to be open all the time, which allowed everyone a chance to participate.'

From this, various teams and competitions emerged, accompanied by the inevitable partisanship and debate on the latest match between DFC Viktoria and Deutschen Spielvereingung, two of the football teams. Swimmers were not ignored and groups of them were a regular sight in the town, as they made their way, towels over their arms, to Dorchester's open-air swimming pool at an area of the River Frome by Grey's Bridge.[163]

Enjoying a swim in Dorchester's outdoor swimming pool at Grey's Bridge. (Courtesy of the Keep Military Museum.)

One sight that Durnovarians and those living in the villages surrounding Dorchester got used to during the war was that of large groups of prisoners venturing into the countryside on exercise marches. For the prisoners it was an opportunity to escape for a while from life inside the barbed wire and see the beautiful landscape. One delegation who visited the camp in early 1915 noted that groups of 200–300 prisoners went on recreational marches

163 Dorchester's swimming pool was built in the early 20th century, when part of the river at Ten Hatches was emptied and the banks were lined with brick. It had a diving board and changing rooms, and remained open until the polio epidemic in the 1950s.

daily. They were observed to be singing and tea awaited them when they got back to the camp.[164] There is a photograph showing one group marching past the Sydney Arms public house in Bridport Road, Dorchester, and one wonders what went through their minds as they returned to their alcohol-free home. At least the Sydney Arms did not have to change its name, as did the Eagle in Holyport, Hampshire. When the local prisoners marched past that particular hostelry they saluted the pub sign, which reminded them of the German national emblem. This did not go down well with the local population, so the name of the pub was changed to the Belgian Arms, and it remains so today.

Prisoners, returning to camp after an exercise march, pass the Sydney Arms in Bridport Road.

Prisoners, in good humour, wave to the photographer recording one of their exercise marches. (Courtesy of the Keep Military Museum.)

164 Naville and Van Bercham's inspection report.

Keeping in Touch

Keeping in touch with home was central to the psyche of the POW. Letters, postcards and parcels provided a link with loved ones and were a constant reminder of a life before their freedom was taken away from them. Sometimes a letter might contain some terrible news, perhaps the death of a loved one, but even so, the appetite for news from home was voracious. The continued receipt of post was important for both the morale of the individual and the prison camp as a whole, and helped maintain good discipline.

Gunther Plüschow described just how important the expectation of mail from home was, when he wrote, 'The post was the Alpha and Omega of our existence. We divided our whole day according to its delivery, and the temper of the camp was regulated by it. Every morning was the same spectacle. When the interpreter arrived with the letters everything was abandoned and forgotten. The English officer was surrounded by a silent crowd of waiting people. Each one's heart was filled with the burning wish to receive some token, some loving wish from home. What joy when one's hopes were fulfilled, how great the disappointment when they were shattered. In the latter case, we always said, "one more day lost". When I went back to Germany and was asked on many sides what one could do to give pleasure to the prisoners, I always said: Write, write as much as you can. What the prisoner longs for most are letters.'[165]

Similar sentiments were expressed in the *Deutsche Blätter*: 'Above all, the current prisoners as well as those newly arrived in the camp longed to send news home to let their families know that they were still alive and also to receive news from home.' This need was recognised by both the German and the British governments who throughout the War put apparatus in place to ensure the free flow of correspondence in and out of camps, and letters certainly flowed at a great rate. Statistics show that the total number of pieces of mail received and sent by UK camps during 1917 was about 13,250,000. In 1918 the figure rose to around 21,250,000.[166]

The right of prisoners to communicate with home was rooted in a 1785 Treaty between the USA and Prussia, and the principle that the cost of postage, including parcels, should be free was established in the Universal Union Postal Convention of 1906. This principle was, however, short lived and from November 1915 letters weighing over 2 oz and parcels sent to and

165 Plüschow.

166 Mark.

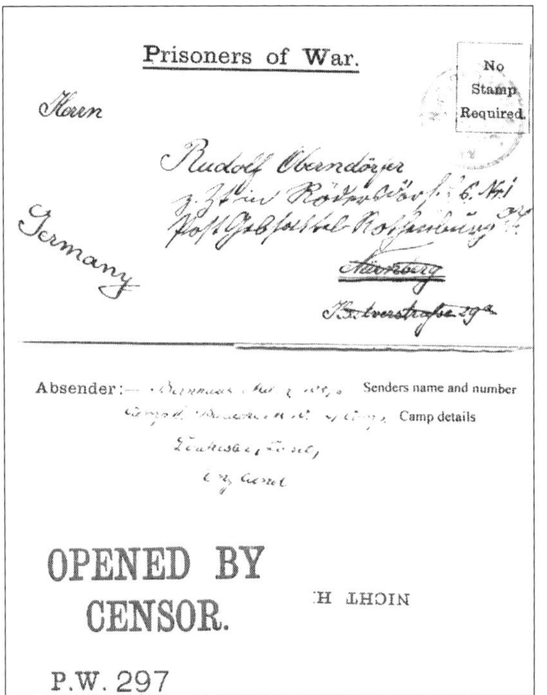

This envelope contained Bernhard Marx's letter to his friend Rudolf Oberndörfer. The front shows that no postage was due and the reverse gives the sender's address[167] *and shows clearly the censor's mark. (Source: P. Dennis.)*

from the Dorchester camp had to be paid for. This was done as a reaction to a decision imposed by the Germans that packages and parcels posted in Germany to prisoners in that country had to be paid for, as did letters and postcards exceeding 50 g.

What prisoners could write and how they wrote it was controlled strictly and subject to precise rules. Early on in the War prisoners wrote their letters on whatever stationery they could get hold of and letters were sent in envelopes. Then, in 1916, a standard, single, foldable sheet of paper was introduced, ruled with 23 lines. This speeded up the whole process because sensors no longer had to read long letters, nor inspect the inside of envelopes. One of the problems censors had was the use by some prisoners of invisible inks. The answer was to give the paper a glossy coating, which made use of such inks difficult. Where possible, letters and postcards had to be written in Latin (Roman) letters, and any written in any other language than English had to have the name of the language written on the outside. Writing between lines was forbidden, as was anything written in pencil and gone over in pen. Plain language had to be used and anything that was considered obscure or curious was especially scrutinised for hidden messages. For the same reason, references to published books, doodles and drawings were not allowed, nor were crosswords, puzzles and musical notation. The men were not allowed postage stamps, in case they wrote a message on the reverse, so, in cases

167 The sender's details are: Bernhard Marx 10875, Compound II, Bauecke (corner building) M10, 27 Camp, Dorchester, Dorset, England.

where they were required to pay postage the stamps were affixed by the camp authorities.

During Naville and Van Bercham's visit to Dorchester a complaint was made that the post was slow. It was pointed out by the camp authorities that it was due to the ingenuity that many prisoners show in the use of 'sympathetic' ink, which they made out of the most diverse substances. This ink, under the influence of heat, revealed quite another text besides that of the ordinary letters. A case was mentioned of one prisoner who gave a sentry £18 to get an uncensored letter through to him, resulting in the two men being sentenced to several months' imprisonment.

Whilst there were some prisoners who tried to break the rules, for most of them the only reason for writing was to exchange news with their loved ones and friends. Men like Bernhard Marx, who wrote to his friend, Rudolf Oberndörfer, 'My dear friend Rudolf! Faithful and faithful. You have not forgotten me, and thought of me by sending numerous letters, cheering me up with your stories, which brought me close to our homeland … I was most interested to hear the story about the Gymnasium[168] and I hope everything turned out well there. I was happy to hear about the message you gave to our minister. I also liked your stories about our Christmas celebrations. Oh, would all our wishes come true, that all of us, who are so far flung throughout the world, could come together under the Christmas tree and enjoy the Christmas message in peace.'[169]

Prisoners were not allowed cameras in the camp, but this did not stop Georg Prell sending a photograph of himself, which had been made into a postcard, to his wife Julia, whilst Martin Pfleiderer gave his family, who lived in Württemberg, some idea of what his life was like by sending a postcard that showed prisoners inside the camp reading room. Interestingly, he also had a photograph of Col Bulkeley, the Camp Commandant. The postcard depicting Prell was taken by the local photographer Charles Furbear, who had his studio at 66 Great Western Road, Dorchester, and must have been one of several who found a ready market for their talents among the prisoners.

Christmas was a time to exchange greetings and in 1917 the prisoners produced their own Christmas card, designed by prisoner Carl Bessinger and probably printed by the camp's printing works. The card depicts an obviously German winter scene of a church and trees covered heavily with snow, and some church bells. On it is written 'I hear the sound of Christmas

168 Equivalent to High School.
169 Letter dated 20/4/1917, in the ownership of P. Dennis.

Christmas card designed by Carl Bessinger.

bells. Dorchester 17'. Another, more personal, greeting card made as a postcard for Christmas 1916 shows a group of about 30 prisoners outside one of the huts, around an elaborately decorated Christmas tree.

The number of letters a prisoner could send was restricted to two per week, except in special circumstances, but the number he could receive was unlimited. In addition, postcards and cards acknowledging the receipt of parcels were allowed. Correspondence with captives in other British camps was forbidden, because of the possibility of conspiracy. Every letter leaving Dorchester had to be scrutinised by a censor. Initially, this job was

Christmas 1916 and 32 prisoners assemble outside their hut, with their highly decorated Christmas tree.

done within the camp, but it was soon realised that the task was far too big to be dealt with locally. Accordingly, the censorship of mail was centralised and carried out by the Prisoners of War Branch of the Postal Censorship, otherwise known as M.I.9 (C) 2. Mail from Dorchester was sent in batches to the organisation's offices in London, where it was always dealt with by the same group of censors. That way the examiner could become familiar with an individual letter writer's background and interests, giving him or her a better chance to recognise anything that was suspicious or out of the ordinary. Lists were kept of certain prisoners whose correspondence had to be paid special attention, which included crews of U-Boats and Zeppelins and senior officers. Letters might also contain some comment about an intended escape or refer to poor conditions or ill-treatment in a camp. In the latter case a note was made and the matter was referred back to the Commandant for action. Incoming post could provide particularly valuable information about the social, military, political and economic state of the enemy, and by cross-referencing little bits of information an accurate picture could be obtained. The import of foreign books was forbidden, unless they were on the permitted list, in which case they were searched for secret messages. Enemy newspapers were not allowed.

If anything was more welcome than a letter from a loved one it was a parcel. The contents of a parcel not only were practical, whether it be a food item or a pair of socks, but also provided the comfort that came with receiving tangible and familiar things from home. Like correspondence, parcels were subject to close examination. These were opened in the camp, in the presence of the prisoner, to negate pilfering. Contraband items, such as alcohol and knives, were confiscated, as were medicines, and the boxes were checked for false bottoms or writing hidden between layers of cardboard. Wrappings were destroyed.

Even with centralised censorship, the job of processing the mail in and out of the Dorchester camp was enormous. Given that the average population over the life of the camp was about 3,000, and that each prisoner could send two letters per week and receive any number, plus postcards, it is not unreasonable to surmise that the amount of mail dealt with by the camp post office exceeded 4,000 pieces each week. According to one report, parcels were arriving at the rate of 2,500 each week,[170] whilst the *Reading Eagle* reported that during the pre-Christmas rush in 1915 they were arriving at the rate of 1,500 per day.[171]

170 *Charleston Sunday News*, 2/1/1916.
171 *Reading Eagle*, 23/1/1916.

Thanks to the *Deutsche Blätter* we have some indication of how the postal service worked; it told its readers: 'The postal area represents for the POWs a central point of the life of the camp. Overseen, of course, by the English, but kept running by the prisoners, it is split into three sections – letters, parcels and monetary post, which are distributed daily at specified times. Letters are gathered up twice a week ... With larger amounts of money sent, for some an account is set up, from which a weekly amount of 10 shillings can be withdrawn. Usually, money and parcels arrive in 2 weeks, whereas letters which come take on average 3–4 weeks.'

Escapes

Any prisoner wanting to escape from the Dorchester camp was faced with a very daunting task. The camp was guarded continuously and floodlit during the hours of darkness. Should the escapee get free of the camp he then had to make his way to a port, preferably on the east coast, in the hope of getting onto a ship that would take him to a neutral country, such as Sweden, Denmark or the Netherlands. Realistically, the best way to make the journey from Dorchester to the coast was by train, with which the town was well provided. The line from Dorchester South terminated at London Waterloo, whilst trains from Dorchester West went to Bristol. The Dorset accent is very distinctive and in a town like Dorchester a stranger asking for rail tickets, especially one with a foreign accent, would arouse suspicion.

Despite the dangers and difficulties, several escape attempts were made from Dorchester. Even though prisoners were generally well looked after and no longer subject to the risk of death and deprivation at the front line, this did not stop men risking their lives by attempting to get home. Motivations to escape may have included the desire to get back and fight for their country, homesickness, or just a way of continuing the war in the enemy's country. The most opportune time to get away was when a prisoner was working on one of the farms around the county. In theory, prisoners working on farms were well guarded, with one guard to every ten prisoners, but, in practice, it was not as simple as that. On larger farms the prisoners might be spread out and left unguarded for periods of time, and there were occasions when they were not guarded at all. Giving evidence during the case of the woman who sold port wine to Germans, Capt. Mitchell, an officer at the camp, told local magistrates that some of the prisoners were allowed to be billeted on some farms without any guard at all, the farmers being responsible for them. In fact, most of the escapes involving Dorchester prisoners seem to have originated from the camp itself.

The first attempt occurred in December 1914 and was reported by the *Chronicle* in an article with the intriguing headline: 'The German Jack in the Box'.[172] The story behind the headline was equally as intriguing and the newspaper described it as being 'Worthy to rank with the famous adventures of Baron Münchausen'. The principal actor was Oberleutnant Otto Koehn, a German who had been taken off the ship *SS Potsdam* at Falmouth on 24

172 *Chronicle*, 14/12/1914. The incident was also reported in the *London Times* on 21/12/1914.

August, whilst making his way back from America to Germany to rejoin the navy. After capture he was sent to Southampton and thence onward to the camp in Dorchester. He took his opportunity to gain freedom when a group of prisoners in the camp, who were above military age, were to be repatriated via Rotterdam and Hamburg.

Among their luggage, on the day of their departure, was an ordinary-looking matchbox packing case, bearing the usual inscription 'Non-Poisonous – Safety Matches'. It was secured by two clasps, one with a padlock and the other with a wooden peg, and it bore the words 'via Hambro'. Men and luggage left Dorchester by train and arrived at Tilbury Docks, via London, on the morning of 12 December, for transfer to the Dutch steamship *SS Batavia V* which was on its way down the River Thames from Custom House Quay. On arrival, the ship anchored in the estuary and the men, with their luggage, were put onto the ferry *Katherine* and duly transferred to the ship. When the porters on the *Batavia V* reached the packing case, they found it far too heavy to lift, so they began to roll it along the whole length of the tender and onto the gangway between the two craft. Then, suddenly, bystanders were surprised to see the arm of a man protruding through the lid and some of the Dutch sailors rushed to Capt. Jerviss, skipper of the *Katherine*, and, pointing to the box, called out in broken English, 'Man inside, man inside!' At first, the captain did not understand what they were saying, but when he saw what was going on he ordered that the lid be forced off.

The man inside was Otto, who was over 6 ft tall and had been incarcerated in his temporary home for over 15 hours. The reported size of the packing case varied, depending on which newspaper report one read, but the *Chronicle* assured its readers that its representative had measured it with a tape and the dimensions were 3 ft long, 2 ft deep and 2 ft wide.[173] Inside the box were fixed loops of rope which Otto could hang on to when the going got rough, and to sustain him on his journey it contained a bottle of meat extract, half a dozen bananas,[174] two champagne bottles containing water and, ingeniously, a rubber pillow filled with oxygen. Another report claimed that the bottles contained cocoa and that there was also a tube containing a mysterious substance. An eyewitness to the moment of Otto's liberation said, 'He was a tall, clean-shaven young fellow, and from his speech and

173 According to another newspaper the box measured 5×3×2 ft 6 ins and contained armrests and a large rug.

174 It seems extraordinary that Otto managed to get hold of bananas, which were not introduced into this country commercially until June 1912. They may well have been sent to him in a food parcel.

appearance, he was well-to-do and well educated. His clothes were good, and he had money. He looked so comical when he came sprawling out on the wet deck that for the moment I could not help laughing.'[175] The *Church Times* described him as 'a distinguished looking young man, with fair hair and a slight fair moustache. He is 21 years old, and wears a pince nez.'[176]

On being discovered, the semi-conscious Otto was extricated from the box and taken to the Captain's cabin, where he was questioned but pretended that he could not speak English. It was only when an immigration official turned up that he admitted that he had a good command of English, but, even so, he declined to make a statement, except to the fact that no one else was involved in the attempt, which could not have been the case as the padlock on the outside of the box was locked.

Otto's next journey was to Gravesend police station, where he was kept until an escort was available to take him back to Dorchester. The *Chronicle* told its readers that Koehn was court-marshalled, although there is no evidence of this ever happening. In fact, he seems to have got off lightly as the only punishment he appears to have been given was a requirement to report each day to the commandant of the camp. Even that did not last for long, because soon after the event, the *Manchester Evening News* reported that among 400 internees transferred from Dorchester to Handforth Camp in Cheshire was the adventurous German Lt Otto Koehn.[177]

Ten months later a second escape was made from the camp, this time by five men. On 16 September 1915, two of them, Josef Strutman and Walther Iven, got clear, although their method of escape is unknown, and made their way to Moreton train station, situated 7 miles to the east of Dorchester. There they bought third class tickets for London, but their journey proved to be a short one, when they were captured at Southampton West by the police, who were searching the train after being alerted. As well as their tickets, the escapees had in their possession £1 13 shillings and a map of the south of England, which had been cut from a book. Iven stated that he belonged to a regiment of Guards, while Strutman said that he was part of a captured U-boat crew.

While all this was happening, back in Dorchester the National Reserve had been called out following a reported sighting of prisoners in Purlings Wood, a few miles to the west of the camp. Another report spoke of three men acting suspiciously at Dorchester South railway station before

175 *Border Watch*, 30/1/1915
176 *The Church Times*, December 1914.
177 *Manchester Evening News*, 10/12/1914.

boarding the early morning train to Waterloo. In any event, the remaining three birds had flown. Two of them were Edwin Bergmann, a 20-year-old soldier, and Hans Heym, a 21-year-old navy pilot. Bergmann had been captured at Ypres and treated in the Connaught Hospital, Aldershot, before removal to Dorchester. Heym was an observer in a Friedrichshafen FF29 seaplane, which, on the night of 21/22 February 1915, passed over the English coast at Clacton and flew on to Braintree, where it dropped two incendiary bombs. On the return flight, he and his pilot dropped a small high-explosive bomb in nearby Coggeshill, and another on Colchester Barracks, which damaged some buildings. The intruders might have made their escape but the plane developed engine trouble and they had to ditch into the sea.

After getting out of the camp, Bergmann and Heym managed to make their way north to Hartlepool docks, where they attempted to find a neutral ship to stow away on. Their plan was thwarted by an observant crane driver by the name of Preston who, seeing them behaving suspiciously, told a local contractor named McFarlane, who also happened to be the Mayor of Hartlepool. He apprehended them, after chasing them on his bicycle, and informed the police. At the police station, the men, who spoke very good English, claimed initially that they were British evangelists going to open a mission, but, when Superintendent McDonald of the local police told them that they would be detained, pending verification, they admitted that they were prisoners of war. The two men appeared before the local magistrates, charged with entering a prohibited area without a pass, and were sentenced to 6 months hard labour. The severity of their sentence was probably influenced by the fact that when they were searched they were found to have London tram tickets on them, showing that they had been travelling around a militarily sensitive area. Among the magistrates at the hearing that day was the very man, the Mayor, who had arrested them. He suggested to the two men that if, indeed, they were evangelists, as they claimed, the only gospel they were going to spread was the gospel of hate. The fate of the fifth man, named Valker, is unknown.

Alarm over the latest escapes went beyond the locality and questions were asked in the House of Commons. Harold Tennant,[178] the Under-Secretary of State for War, in answer to a question put by Henry Craik,[179] informed the House that investigations were taking place after the spate of escapes

178 Harold 'Jack' Tennant (1865–1935), Scottish Liberal MP for Berwickshire.

179 Sir Henry Craik, 1st Baronet, PC, KCB (1846–1927), Scottish Unionist MP, Glasgow and Aberdeen Universities.

from the Dorchester camp. It was suggested that prisoners should wear more distinctive clothing.

Despite the change in personnel, escapes from Dorchester did not stop. In February 1916 an article in the *Taunton Courier*[180] was headed 'DORCHESTER GERMANS RECAPTURED – A GOOD TIME IN LONDON – FOUND IN NEW CLOTHES & WITH ENGLISH GOLD'. This intriguing headline referred to a little jaunt made by Lt Von Schweiniken and Private Pohmer, who had escaped a week before their recapture. Von Schweiniken had been awarded the Iron Cross after the Battle of Mons and was repudiated to be related to the Prince of Bismarck[181]. Both were caught in London, and when Detective-Sergeant Cox of the Special Branch of Scotland Yard arrested Pohmer, the prisoner made no attempt to run off but went quietly in a taxi to Cannon Row police station. Two hours later, Von Schweiniken was apprehended by Sgt Cox and another officer in Leicester Square. Evidently, the prisoner was not hard to identify as he walked with a pronounced limp caused by eight bullet wounds in his leg and thigh. According to the *Courier*, both men seemed thoroughly contented with their 5 days of liberty and confessed that they had had a pleasurable time. They claimed to have had plenty of money on them, a number of gold sovereigns were found in their possession, and they declared that they had dined at West End restaurants and moved freely around the city.

The men had made their escape during a performance in the camp theatre. Seizing their opportunity, they bound old pieces of sacking about them and covered their hands to prevent them being torn by the barbed-wire, and after forcing their way through the wire they headed for London. At some stage they disposed of their uniforms and got hold of two grey suits. Having got to the Capital they faced a major problem, that of finding accommodation, because new regulations had been introduced, requiring those persons staying in hotels and boarding houses to register. Their solution was simple; they made friends with some women who entertained them at their homes. Both men were escorted back to Dorchester for Court Martial.

On 25 October 1916 the *Liverpool Echo* informed its readers that a German POW, formerly a London waiter, had escaped from the Dorchester internment camp. He was described by Scotland Yard as being 5 ft 7 in tall, of fair complexion and with a scar on the left side of his neck. He was wearing a German army uniform and spoke good English.

Another prisoner, Frederick Goettling, aged 28, featured in the following

180 *Taunton Courier and Advertiser*, 16/2/1916.
181 Otto Eduard Leopold, Prince of Bismarck, Duke of Lauenburg (1815–1898).

article in the *Taunton Courier*[182] after he attempted to get back home: 'RE-CAPTURED HUN – ESCAPED FROM DORCHESTER AND FOUND IN WEST SOMERSET – On Monday morning a German POW, who had escaped from the Dorchester Internment Camp, gave himself up to the West Somerset police at Stogumber. He was brought to Williton Police Station, where in answer to PC Woolley, he stated that his name was Frederick Goettling; aged 28, a commercial clerk, and he resided in London prior to the war. He had escaped on the previous Tuesday, and from an itinerary in his possession, and on his own admission, he had endeavoured to reach Bristol, where he hoped to get away in a neutral vessel. In effecting his escape, he met with a spike wound in the thigh, and the police had him medically attended while awaiting an escort. He wore his camp uniform, covered with a mackintosh, and had 2s.3d. on him. He was captured at Ypres in March last.'

The last and most tragic escape attempt from Dorchester occurred after the War had ended. At an inquest held on Saturday 17 May 1919 in one of the hospital huts at the camp, the Coroner for South Dorset, Mr G.P. Symes, heard evidence concerning the death of a young prisoner who had apparently tried to cut through the barbed wire of the camp. The man concerned was a 21-year-old Polish soldier named Franz Radgowski, who paid the ultimate price for his desperation.

Lt Samuel Conroy of the 5th Btn, King's Royal Rifles, informed the coroner that he was the officer in charge of the guard on the night of 16 May 1919. At 12.45 am he heard two shots and ran out to the area where they had apparently come from. There he found two sentries, Riflemen Ramplin and Wilson, and a body lying on the ground near the barbed wire fence. Asked what had happened, Wilson said that he saw the man cutting the wire, and despite being challenged by both he and Ramplin he did not stop, so they fired at him. This resulted in the arrival of the sergeant of the guard who found a man rolling around, near the latrines. Lt Conroy loosened the prisoner's clothing and found that he had been shot in the abdomen. By now a number of prisoners had come to their hut doors to see what was going on and one of them, Heinrich Dauster, came forward and spoke to the man, asking him why he had tried to cut the wire, to which Radgowski replied, 'Because I wished to go home.' He was then taken to the camp hospital, where a search of his clothing revealed a pair of wire cutters.

Pte Frederick Wilson informed the jury that, on the night in question, he

182 *Taunton Courier and Advertiser*, 8/11/1916.

was on guard when he heard a shout of 'Halt'. He went round to Ramplin who told him to keep an eye out as he thought there was a German in the wire. A quarter of an hour later they both heard a noise that sounded like someone trying to cut or break it. Both men approached the sound and saw a man lying face down in the wire. Wilson put his rifle to his shoulder and shouted 'Halt.' Radgowski began to get up and it was at that point that Wilson shot him. Despite this, the prisoner ran towards the camp and was again shot, this time by Ramplin.

The camp medical officer, Maj. William Burrough Cosens, stated that Radgowski had entered the camp in October 1918 and had been healthy up until the time of his death, which took place within 20 minutes of his arrival at the hospital. He consequently carried out a post mortem on the body and came to the conclusion that he had been shot in the back, the bullet then passing through his body and through his hand. He said that the angle of entry into the body indicated that the prisoner had been kneeling down when he was shot. After hearing the evidence, the jury returned a verdict of justifiable homicide.

Despite the fate of Franz Radgowski, there were further escape attempts. Perhaps the prisoners felt that as the War was over the penalties would not be severe, or that the authorities would not bother to look for them. The *Yorkshire Post and Leeds Intelligencer* reported, on 25 August 1919, that Otto Kempe, a sailor captured from the German merchant raider *SMS Greif*,[183] got free, but his fate is not known. A week earlier, the same newspaper told of Wilhelm Holling's recapture, following his premature departure from Dorchester. It was a busy time for escapees; in the same week, five prisoners sought freedom from Abbey Dore Workhouse in Ross-on-Wye and one from Brocton Camp in Staffordshire.

183 *SMS Greif*, a converted cargo ship, engaged with the British armed merchant cruiser *HMS Alcantaras* on 29 February 1916. Both ships were sunk and there were 210 German survivors.

The Guards

The *Chronicle* tells us that the first batch of prisoners to arrive in Dorchester was escorted by a contingent of Scottish Fusiliers,[184] and it was they who formed the first guard at the camp. However, as regular, trained-for-combat troops, their priorities lay elsewhere and it was not long before they were replaced.

On 25 September 1914 the *Western Gazette* reported that the local Mobilisation Committee[185] had been called upon to raise two companies from the National Reserve, 2nd Class,[186] to relieve the troops guarding the German prisoners, and that they would commence their duties as soon as clothing could be provided for them. It was informed that each company would be made up of three officers, five sergeants, five corporals, two drummers, plus 110 rank and file, and they would form part of the Reserve (Home Service) 4th Btn of the Dorsetshire Rgt.

Enlistment was for 1 year or the duration of the war, and if the war was over in less than 1 year the men were to be discharged with all convenient speed. All enlistments would be in the rank of private, promotions being made after final approval. Each man would receive a bounty of £5, providing he registered immediately, and pay and conditions were to be those of the Territorial Force.

When it came to accommodating this addition to the town's population, the Committee decided to ask for permission to erect huts near the prison camp. Two weeks later, the *Western Gazette* was able to report that 'Excellent progress was made in raising the required quota for National Reservists of the 2nd Class, to relieve the Royal Scots Fusiliers, in the guarding of the German prisoners. On Saturday 29 September the men who had so far

184 *Chronicle*, 27/8/1914.

185 The Mobilisation Committee was a committee of the Dorset Territorial Association. The Association, which was set up in 1908, administered the Dorsetshire Rgt Territorial Force and was located in Dorchester. The Chairman was normally the Deputy Lieutenant and the rest of the committee was made up of military representatives and elected councillors. Chairman of the Dorset Association was Lt Col John Mount Batten of Up Cerne, who lost his son John on 25 October 1914, shot through the heart by a German sniper.

186 The National Reserve was a list of trained officers and men who were no longer required to serve in the military. Its purpose was to enable an increase in military resources in the event of imminent national danger. The lists were kept by the County Associations, who were responsible for maintaining the lists and recruiting and organising the units in their area. The National Reserve, 2nd Class, comprised men between the ages of 40 and 55 who had served in the ranks and sergeants up to 55.

proffered their services assembled at Dorchester, to the number of about 175, and billets were found for them in the town. On Monday morning a party of about 70, one man from each billet, were drawn up in the front of the Shire Hall and County House, where they were given their orders.

The men have not yet got their uniforms but they will be supplied as soon as possible. Huts are to be built shortly in Colliton Park for the accommodation of the men. They will be of galvanised iron, and tenders for their erection are already being asked for. There are two parades every day for drill on the barrack square. The numbers will, we anticipate, soon be made up to full compliment.

Maj. D. Hughes-Onslow,[187]of Colliton House, Dorchester, was to have commanded the National Reserve Prison Guard, but he has been transferred to the 6th Btn, Dorset Rgt, in camp at Worgret. Thereupon, his place was filled by the appointment of Capt. H. Aubrey Cartwright, of Upwood, Sixpenny Handley. The other officers who have been appointed are Capt. D.C. Greenlees, of Parkstone: Lts B.A. Bloxome, of Weymouth; R.J. Gollop, of Beaminster; H.B. Legg, of Litton Cheney; J.M. Rossiter, of Marnhull; and H.R. Yorke, of Broadwindsor.'

By 9 October only a few more men were required to fill the two companies, and a week after that the quota had been met. Training began in earnest, the men exercising daily, but they still had no uniforms. Instead, they were issued with red armbands marked conspicuously with the letters N.R. in black.

Those Reservists assigned to the camp finally took up their duties on Wednesday 14 October, with a contingent of the Cornwall National Reserve

Group photograph of guards posing in front of parts of the ramparts of Poundbury hill fort. (Source: S. Flowers.)

187 Denzil Hughes-Onslow was a well-known local figure. On the outbreak of war he and his wife gave over their home to the Red Cross, to be used as a military hospital, which operated throughout the war and cared for 2006 men. See also page 56.

brought in to help their Dorset comrades,[188] replacing a contingent of the 3rd Btn Royal Scottish Regiment.[189]

As for their accommodation, the wooden huts were never built in Colliton Park, or elsewhere. Instead, a camp of bell tents was established, which stretched from the western edge of the prison camp up onto Poundbury hill fort. The tents were exposed to the weather and life for the soldiers must have been very uncomfortable during the winter. It was certainly not the best place for those guards who found themselves in the camp because their health prevented them from fighting. This inappropriate accommodation came to national attention when the German government complained that prisoners at Dorchester were still being housed in tents during the winter. To establish the truth, representatives of the Red Cross visited the camp and found that, whilst the captives were accommodated in heated huts, supplied with electricity, their guards were living in tents. One of the delegation, an American, was overheard to say, 'By Jove, the English treat their prisoners well.'[190]

These two photographs show the guards' camp. The top one was one of a series taken of the prison guards' camp by Hills and Rowney of 23 High West Street, Dorchester. (Courtesy of the Keep Military Museum.) The lower one shows the extent of the guards' camp which ran up the slopes of Poundbury hill fort. It was hardly the most hospitable place to be sleeping in tents.

188 *Western Gazette*, 9/10/1914.
189 This reference to the Royal Scots Rgt contradicts the *Chronicle's* earlier reference to the Scots Fusiliers guarding the prisoners. It is likely that the former reference is correct, as the 3rd Scots Rgt was stationed locally in Weymouth in August 1914.
190 *Chronicle*, 25/12/1915.

Members of the National Reserve were not the only class of soldiers to guard prisoners at the camp. In August 1917 the Royal Defence Corps (RDC) was established from the home battalions of certain regiments, and consisted of men who were too old or unfit medically to fight at the Front. They were assigned tasks at home, like guarding important features such as ports, railways and bridges, and guarding prisoners of war. Then, there were men like James Butts, who found himself in Dorchester after escorting a group of prisoners from the Western Front with the 78 POW Company.[191] Others, like Fred Green and George Squibb, were local men who wanted to do their bit for the War effort.

In the early months of 1918 several of the RDC units were disbanded and the guarding of prisoners was, once again, taken over by regular regiments. In May 1919, when Franz Radgowski was shot,[192] the 5 Btn King's Royal Rifles were guarding the prisoners.

Boredom must have been as much a problem for guards as it was for the prisoners, and to help combat it a number of diversions were provided for them. For example, there were sporting events. On a Monday in June 1916, local residents assembled at Poundbury to witness a tug of war between teams of sergeants of the RDC and Other Ranks. There were also races, at which Pte Rodway shone, and all this took place whilst the RDC band, under the conductorship of Band Sgt Honey, entertained the assembled crowd with a variety of music.

As early as October 1914, the Town Council felt that it had some responsibility for entertaining the troops garrisoned in the town, a sentiment that extended to the prison guards.[193] In 1915 it decided to provide a recreation hut for them, to be sited at their camp, funded by the YMCA and local donations. When it was opened in January 1916, the *Western Gazette* described the event in some detail: 'Although not wholly completed, the new Y.M.C.A. hut, which has been erected near the Poundbury Concentration Camp for the use of the National Reservists of the Prison Guard, was opened on Friday afternoon with becoming ceremony. The hut is not erected within the actual confines of the camp itself, but on a site quite adjacent, kindly granted by Mr R.S. Hunt of Poundbury Farm, and Major Worth, the Camp Commandant, has kindly consented to the erection being placed in bounds for the full use and enjoyment of the men of the guard. The hut measures 63 feet long, 20 feet broad and 18 feet in height to the ridge. The structure

191 See page 125.

192 See page 109.

193 *Western Gazette*, 16/10/1914.

is constructed of red deal, weather-boarded, match lined, and roofed with Canadian galvanised tiles. The windows are large and numerous, which makes the hut light and sunny in pleasant weather. By night it is illuminated adequately with oil. At the further end is a convenient buffet, and at the back two bedrooms for the caretakers, plus a kitchen and office.'[194] By March 1916 the interior had been varnished and decorated with pictures, the local newspaper commenting that, 'it now presents a most comfy and cosy appearance'.[195]

The varnish was barely dry when the first entertainment was organised, a performance by the Frampton Family Band, and after that concerts and entertainments were held on a regular basis. In July 1916, the Framptons made a return visit, as part of a programme that included Mr W. Dampier, who gave a bright address, Miss May Allen, with her vocal solos, and a violinist, Mr Sewell. Performances were not confined to music and singing. On one occasion, Sgt Maj. J.M. Moody, a veteran of the Seaforth Highlanders, told a packed audience of his exploits serving under Lord Roberts in Afghanistan, with Lord Wolsely at Tel-el-Kabir in Egypt, and of his life as a missionary in South Africa during the Boer War. In March 1916 a very enjoyable evening was spent by the guards when Miss Barbara Cozen's group of Pierrettes gave a 'bright and varied' programme of songs and dances, the best of which, according to the reporter present, were the dancing of the Irish Jig and the song 'The Only, Only Way', both receiving 'vociferous encores'.[196] It appears that the guards also had talent within their own ranks. On several occasions, Quartermaster Sgt King was asked to sing at local events, including a Red Cross concert in the village of Evershot. Neither were the men's spiritual needs ignored. During the life of the hut, mission concerts and religious meetings were held there often.

Of course, unlike the POWs, the soldiers of the guard had access to the town, which during the War provided all kinds of entertainment and diversions. Concerts and soirees were held in the Corn Exchange, often to raise funds for all manner of good causes, like the Dorset Regiment Comforts Fund. Very popular in the summer were the Sunday afternoon concerts given by military bands in the town's Borough Gardens, and if a guard wanted the latest news on the progress of the War he could visit the Electric Picturedrome, Dorchester's cinema, located in Durngate Street. In July 1915, audiences were treated to a film showing the life of a sailor in the

194 *Western Gazette*, 28/1/1916.
195 *Western Gazette*, 3/3/1916.
196 *Western Gazette*, 24/3/1916.

This amusing photograph of a group of guards reflects the fact that some of them were not fit enough to serve at the Front. Pte Frederick Tibbs'[198] *head is to the left of the guard holding the teapot. (Source: S. Flowers.)*

Royal Naval Division.[197]

Perhaps because it was a garrison town full of soldiers, Dorchester had a strong anti-alcohol lobby, led by the ladies of the Dorchester United Church of England Temperance Society, who ran a coffee room in the Corn Exchange which was very popular with the troops. Another alcohol-free establishment was the Soldiers' Home and Institute in North Square, which was opened in 1888 to provide an alternative to the public house as a place where soldiers could relax. It had a coffee bar, reading room, library, bathrooms and a recreation and smoking room. The soldiers' spiritual needs were met by gospel and temperance meetings, which were held nearly every night in the mission rooms. However, for many off-duty soldiers it was the local public houses, like the Ship Inn in High West Street, a favourite with soldiers, that

197 Opened on 24 April 1911, the Electric Picturedrome was Dorchester's first full-time cinema. In 1920 it was refurbished and reopened as The Palace. It showed its last film on 4 May 1957 and was demolished in the 1970s. The site is now occupied by flats, appropriately named Palace Court.

198 See page 120.

provided the main attraction, and, soldiers being soldiers, some of the guards found themselves on the wrong side of the law, due often to over-imbibing.

One offender was George Spicer, a private in the RDC, who was summoned for using obscene language in St Martin's Road[199] on 27 February 1919. In his defence, an officer from the prison camp stated that the defendant had been a POW in Germany for nearly 3 years. He had been guarding the German prisoners for about 3 weeks, and was an excellent soldier. Unfortunately, he added, some of the repatriated soldiers met up with so-called friends, with the result that they sometimes had too much to drink and forgot themselves, as the defendant had apparently done. Spicer was fined 10 shillings.

Guard Pte Frederick Day appeared before the police court for being found drunk and disorderly one afternoon in Cornhill. The defendant's excuse was that he had a bad cold, for which he had taken a small whisky, which accounted for the trouble. He was fined 5 shillings, plus 5 shillings for the cost of a doctor, whom he insisted should examine him.

Pte John Gleeson was charged with stealing six shirts belonging to Mr H.C. Bailey. He was caught in North Square with a parcel under his arm, and claimed to have been given them, but after enquiries it was established that they had be taken from outside Baileys outfitters in High East Street. Gleeson was reported as saying, 'This is not the first time I have suffered for others, and I can do it again.'[200] He then went on to claim that he had done the deed in a drunken fit, suggesting that it was an opportunist crime. However, Superintendent King put some doubt on that defence when he told the court that the accused had twenty previous convictions.

Another case was somewhat bizarre. A Mrs Selby of 13 South Western Cottages was walking her dog in August 1918, when the animal went missing. A month later, Pte David Anderson was seen carrying the dog out of the prison camp and, when interviewed by the police some days later, claimed that he had found it in the street and taken it to his home in London. He then changed his story, saying that he had found the dog in the prison camp compound after its former owner, a Sergeant Major, had left. The case was dismissed but Anderson had to pay his own costs.

If the former case was bizarre, then another involving a prison guard was very serious. James Hogg was charged with committing indecent assault on a girl aged 5 years, Miss Hilda Symes of Holloway Road, at 6.30 pm one evening, by the river bank near Grey's Bridge. Miss Millicent Mears

---

199 St Martin's Road ran from Top o' Town to the water tower. It is now known as Bridport Road.
200 *Western Gazette*, 14/1/1916.

reported that she was coming back from a walk by the river when she saw the prisoner sitting on the bank with two children, a boy and a girl, near him. The girl appeared frightened and was crying, so she went to the police station and reported it. Hogg was later arrested in the Royal Oak public house. The young private of the 3rd Btn Royal Scots Fusiliers was put on remand, but after the witnesses confirmed their depositions and the girl made a statement, the charge was reduced to one of common assault, to which the prisoner pleaded guilty. The mayor, reprimanding Hogg severely, said that for a man wearing His Majesty's uniform there could be no greater disgrace than his position, and no doubt he was thoroughly ashamed of himself and that this should be a warning to him for the rest of his life. He was given the option of paying a fine of 20 shillings plus costs or being sent to jail for a month.[201]

The desire to get away from the camp was not confined to the prisoners. At the Dorchester Police Court on 6 September 1919, Pte Charles Webster was charged with stealing a bicycle from the village of Charminster.[202] The prisoner had been detained at Cerne Abbas, 8 miles away, as an absentee. He told the Court that he had borrowed the bike to get to the next village and he intended to give it up. He had escaped from the guard room at the prison camp and hidden the bike in a shed at Cerne. Giving evidence, an officer from the camp said Webster had committed several military offences, and Sgt Hayward of the local police added that the man had also been convicted of larceny and four minor offences in Grimsby. Desertion was considered to be a serious offence and the convicted man was sentenced to 6 months' hard labour.

Pte Bertie Gates was another absentee who, according to an officer of his battalion, had been guarding prisoners at the camp for some considerable time and then disappeared on 1 September 1919. He was arrested by PC Symes, in St Thomas Street, Weymouth, 3 weeks later. Symes was awarded 5 shillings by the bench for his efforts.

201 *Western Gazette*, 21/8/1914.
202 Charminster is situated 2 miles north of Dorchester.

Some of the Men Who Served at the Camp

Unfortunately, it has only been possible to find details of a few of the men who served at the camp in Dorchester. The biographies which follow give some indication of why some of the guards and medical orderlies ended up there and what happened to them subsequently. There were at least four deaths among the guards, all of whom were buried in Fordington Cemetery, as were the prisoners who died, plus those servicemen who took their last breath in one of the town's VAD hospitals. Presumably, the families of the allied dead could not afford to have their bodies brought home.

Pte James Lugg – 5026
Dorsetshire Rgt – Dorset National Reserve

On Christmas Day 1914, James Lugg, one of the National Reserve guarding the prisoners at Poundbury Camp, complained of feeling ill and was admitted to the Red Cross Hospital at 6 Church Street, opposite Wollaston House. He was attended by doctors Walker and Gowering but, despite rallying for a time, relapsed and died of heart trouble on 25 January, aged 49. Once again, there followed an impressive military funeral, which the *Chronicle* described to its readers in detail. His body was taken to the mortuary at the County Hospital and on the day of his burial no less than 160 members of the Dorset and Cornwall National Reserve were lined up waiting to accompany his body on its journey to Fordington Cemetery. The procession took the longer route down High West Street to London Road, to avoid the possibility of the horses slipping on the steep gradient of Fordington High Street.

The son of Catherine Lugg, James came from Bere Regis where he worked as a butcher's lad, probably for Joseph Kellaway, the village butcher. At the age of 21 he enlisted into the Army, serving with the Transport Corps for 12 years, and during that period he married Mary Ann Turner in Farnham, Surrey, possibly while he was posted at Aldershot. After his discharge from the Army, James took Mary back to Dorset, where they lived in the village of Wool and had five children. At the time of his death they were living at Littlemoor, a suburb of Weymouth.

Pte George Williams – 20050
Royal Warwickshire Rgt

George Williams found himself in Dorchester as one of the men guarding the German prisoners at Poundbury. In the winter of 1915/16, he was admitted to the military hospital where he died of the very painful Bright's disease[203] on 4 February 1916, aged 45. George came from Birmingham but was buried locally in Fordington. He left behind a widow and three children.

Pte Frederick Tibbs – 24587
Royal Defence Corps

Pte Tibbs was a family man from Napton near Rugby in Warwickshire, where he was employed at the local cement works. On 9 September 1914 he went to the recruiting office to enlist, where he was medically examined and found to be physically fit to serve, despite being laid up for 15 weeks the previous winter. He became a driver in the Amy Service Corps, but it was not long before his poor health put him into hospital, where he was diagnosed with nephritis[204] and rheumatism. An Army Medical Board at Aldershot was told that Fredcrick suffered from continual pain in his back and legs and that his heart was dilated and enlarged. As a consequence he was discharged.

Frederick Tibbs. (Source: S. Flowers.)

Having been invalided out of the Army, Frederick joined the RDC and was posted to Dorchester. On 21 July 1916, he complained of feeling ill and appeared to be in great pain. He was seen by the Medical Officer at the military hospital in the Depot Barracks and died soon after. The police were called

203 A generic term for diseases of the kidneys, which could be described in modern medicine as acute or chronic nephritis.
204 A disease of the kidneys.

as a matter of course and PC Payne, after gathering all the facts, laid them before the Coroner who ordered a post-mortem, which found that he had died of disease of the heart and other organs. He was aged 42.

During the course of the War, Dorchester saw many impressive military funerals but Frederick's must have been an especially moving sight. As well as the usual firing party, military band, funeral bier and carriages of mourners, the procession was followed in the rear by 80 soldiers of his Company. The whole procession moved slowly and solemnly down the High Street to the tune of Handel's Dead March from 'Saul', on its way to Fordington Cemetery where he was buried.

Pte Thomas Meagher[205] – 75522
Royal Defence Corps

Thomas hailed from Shadwell in London and served with the Royal Fusiliers before joining the RDC, presumably because he became unfit for active service. He might have been allocated work nearer to his home but instead was sent to Dorchester to guard German prisoners. The prison camp, where a large number of men were living on top of one another, provided the perfect environment for the influenza epidemic of 1918 to spread, and in October of that year several Germans became victims.

In November, Thomas succumbed and died in the County Hospital on the 10th, aged 41. His death was followed 3 days later by yet another military funeral making its way through the town. As was usual, the cortege was led by the firing party, marching with arms reversed, followed, in this case, by the band of the Salvation Army, no military band being available at the time. Next came the coffin, escorted by six bearers in uniform, and then the carriage carrying the mourners. Bringing up the rear was a large contingent of Thomas's colleagues from the RDC.

Rifleman Reuben Isaacson – 31091
(known in Dorchester as Reuben Ison)
9 Btn, Rifle Bde

Reuben Isaacson was born in West Ham in the East End of London in 1898, His parents were Louis, who had been born in Poland, and Margaret, also

205 Thomas served in the Army under the name of Mears.

known as Annie, who originated from the Isle of Man. Louis worked as a labourer and his wife was employed as a midwife. Margaret was certainly a very good advertisement for her profession, giving birth to no less than fifteen children. Reuben attended West Ham Boys School and when he left the Head Teacher wrote the following testimonial for prospective employers: 'He is a lad of much intelligence and has worked successfully. He is honest, trustworthy, willing and obedient, trustful and painstaking. His general conduct has always been excellent.'[206] Armed with such an exemplary reference he found employment as a junior ledger clerk.

Reuben was not eligible for enlistment into the Army until December 1916, but he joined up underage, on 2 June, giving his age as 18. It appears that the authorities found out about this because he had to re-enlist on 22 January 1917. His medical record shows that his height was 5 ft 8½ in, he weighed 8 st 8 lb and was found to be medically A1. He was put into the 9th Btn, Rifle Brigade, and after initial training joined them in France on 13 April 1917, and probably fought in the Battle of Langemarck and the first and second conflicts at Passchendaele in Belgium.

In the spring of 1918 the young soldier received distressing news from home that his father was very ill and he was granted compassionate leave to return to England. However, his plans were interrupted by the Battle of St Quentin, part of the massive German Spring Offensive, which almost overran allied forces on several parts of the Western Front. The battle commenced on 21 March and on the 23rd the battalion diary recorded that the situation was very serious, with the 9th Btn fighting a rear-guard action. It was on that day that Reuben was reported missing and his family was duly informed. In fact he had been captured by the enemy and for the time being his part in the fighting had come to an end. Sadly, he never saw his father again, who died in 1918.

The first news that Louis and Margaret heard of their son's whereabouts probably came in the postcard he sent them on 16 May, from Standal POW camp, situated 100 km to the west of Berlin. In it he informed them that he was neither ill nor wounded and asked his mother to send a parcel as soon as possible. His next postcard was of a different tone. In it he says, 'I am now at another camp. I am quite well. The work I am doing is very hard but I am sticking to it as well as I can.' Clearly, Reuben had a tough time in Germany and the extent of the severity of his treatment was assessed by a medical board back in England, after he was repatriated on 11 November 1918. The

206 Letter shown to me by a relative.

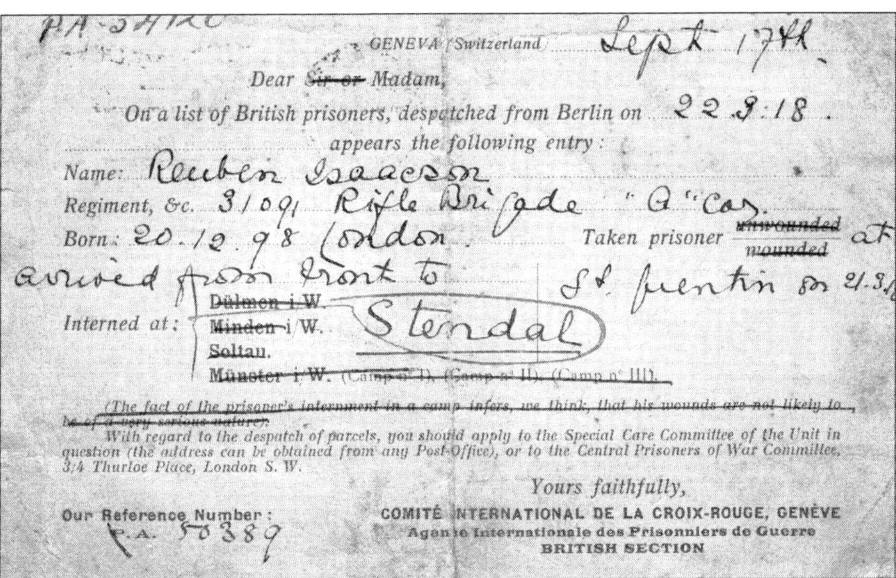

GENEVA (Switzerland) Sept 17th.

Dear ~~Sir or~~ Madam,

On a list of British prisoners, despatched from Berlin on 22.9.18.

appears the following entry:

Name: Reuben Isaacson

Regiment, &c. 31091 Rifle Brigade "A" Coy.

Born: 20.12.98 London. Taken prisoner ~~unwounded~~ ~~wounded~~ at

arrived from front to St. Quentin on 21.3.1[illegible]

Interned at: ~~Dülmen i.W.~~ ~~Minden~~ i/W. Stendal
Soltau.
~~Münster i. W. (Camp n° I), (Camp n° II), (Camp n° III).~~

~~(The fact of the prisoner's internment in a camp infers, we think, that his wounds are not likely to be of a very serious nature).~~

With regard to the despatch of parcels, you should apply to the Special Care Committee of the Unit in question (the address can be obtained from any Post-Office), or to the Central Prisoners of War Committee, 3/4 Thurloe Place, London S. W.

Yours faithfully,

Our Reference Number: P.A. 50389

COMITÉ INTERNATIONAL DE LA CROIX-ROUGE, GENÈVE
Agence Internationale des Prisonniers de Guerre
BRITISH SECTION

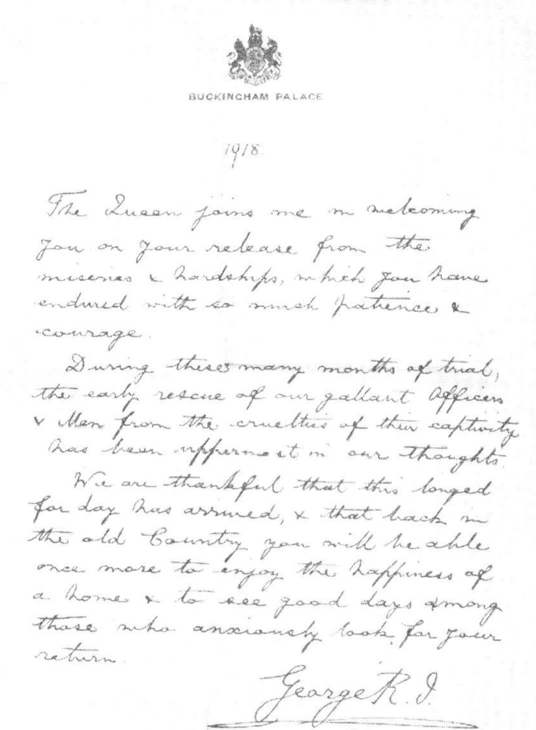

BUCKINGHAM PALACE

1918.

The Queen joins me in welcoming you on your release from the miseries & hardships, which you have endured with so much patience & courage.

During these many months of trial, the early rescue of our gallant Officers & Men from the cruelties of their captivity has been uppermost in our thoughts.

We are thankful that this longed for day has arrived, & that back in the old Country you will be able once more to enjoy the happiness of a home & to see good days among those who anxiously look for your return.

George R.I.

Above: Notification by the International Red Cross in Switzerland of Reuben Isaacson's capture and imprisonment in Stendal prison camp. (Source J. Parker.)
Left: Letter to Reuben Isaacson from King George V, welcoming him home after his captivity in Germany. (Source: J. Parker.)

medical officer found that he was suffering from neurasthenia, akin to shellshock. Reuben's symptoms were weakness, excessive sweating of the palms and a lack of confidence. He also returned with scabies, for which he spent 9 days in hospital.

When Reuben arrived home, a letter was waiting for him from Buckingham Palace, handwritten and apparently signed by the King himself.

Bearing in mind his physical and mental state, plus the fact that the war had ended, one might imagine that Reuben was discharged, but no, instead he was sent to Dorchester as a prison guard.

Finally, he left the Army on 19 October 1919, but not before an appearance before another medical board, this time to assess his eligibility for a pension. It was judged that he was 20% disabled and he was granted a pension of 8 shillings per week. Fortunately, Reuben recovered from the obvious physical and mental effects of his experiences in the war, but, like so many others, the inner scars remained for the rest of his life. His daughter told me that he sometimes cried out during his sleep, reliving his experiences.

Reuben Isaacson (centre front), with other guards, taken at the Dorchester camp. (Source: J. Parker.)

Despite his reason for being in the town, Dorchester obviously made a good impression on Reuben, because in 1939 he brought his family to live there, to escape the expected bombing in London. But he returned to the town with a different name, that of Ison, which the family had changed in 1936. The change came out of fear, because it was the time when the British Union of Fascists were stirring up anti-Jewish feeling in the East End of London, leading to riots and violence. The irony was that the family, despite their name, were not Jewish. During WW2, Reuben served his country again in Dorchester, this time as an air raid warden. He became a well-known and popular resident, particularly in the areas of amateur dramatics and operatics, and was an accomplished sketch artist. Reuben died in 1983.

Pte James Butts – 24914
14 Btn Worcestershire Rgt

Officially James Butts should not have been in the Worcestershire Rgt. Standing at just 5 ft 2½ in, he was half an inch under the regulation height to enter a regular battalion.[207] Despite this, he was duly welcomed into the regiment when he volunteered, and enlisted at Worcester on 25 October 1915, at the age of 36. Why he chose to enlist at that particular time is unknown, but it may well have been in response to a renewed recruitment drive on the part of the Worcesters who were looking for men to fill the ranks of a new battalion that was to have a very specific role in France. The 14th (Service) Btn, known as the Severn Valley Pioneers, was created on 10 September 1915 as a non-combat labour unit. They were looking for men who had construction experience, to build roads, railways and trenches, and James, who was a labourer, was just the man for the job.

James Butts. (Source: D. Butts.)

Having passed his medical he spent the first 8 months of his war with the 6th (Reserve) Btn, doing basic training and learning the skills that his new job required. After training, he was posted to France and arrived at Le Havre on 26 June 1916, just 5 days after the 14th Btn had disembarked there. James joined his unit in the area of Vimy Ridge, Nord-Pas-de-Calais, where he worked on the defences until 3 November, when, for some unknown reason, he returned to the UK for a period of 6 months. Then, it was back to France to rejoin his battalion. His destination this time was Arras, where he was about to become a fighting soldier.

On the first day of the Battle of Arleux,[208] James's platoon were working on roads to the rear and heard the roar of the guns and then saw the lines of wounded men streaming back from the fighting. As darkness fell he went

207 At the time of James's enlistment, men had to be under 40 years of age and over 5 ft 3 in in height.
208 The Battle of Arleux took place on 28 and 29 April 1917, one of a number of battles which were part of an allied offensive during that spring.

back to his quarters to settle down for the night, but not for long. At 9 pm an alarm came, with orders to move forward in fighting order to assist troops in the front line. The enemy were making counter attacks and the battalions were hard pressed. James was issued with ammunition, but there was not time to even think about handing around rations. Through the darkness the 14th marched towards Gavrelle, where it was split up and attached to other units. The men fought among the combat battalions throughout the battle and lost one officer and two Other Ranks and 11 men were wounded.

Next, something happened that would eventually send James away from the Western Front for good. The Army decided that he was not fit enough for labouring anymore and on 2 June 1917 he was attached to the 78th POW Company, which was guarding German POWs at Rouen. It was whilst he was there that he was punished for talking to some prisoners and he lost 3 days' pay. Then, luck favoured him when, on 4 April 1918, he was part of a detachment of the 78th that was given the task of escorting some of the captives to the camp at Dorchester, and there he stayed until September 1918. He then rejoined the Worcestershire Rgt, this time the 1st Garrison Btn which was stationed in Dublin. He was finally discharged on 17 August 1919 and awarded a disability pension because he was found to be suffering from myalgia and rheumatism, as a result of his war service.

Pte William Thomas – 236
1/4th Btn Dorsetshire Rgt

When war came, William Thomas was already very familiar with the Army. Born in 1869 at Burton, near the village of Wool in Dorset, he joined the Dorset Rifle Volunteers at the age of 16, and when the force became part of the new Territorial Army in 1908, he continued to re-enlist each year until 1914, when he joined the 1/4th Btn Dorsets, aged 45.

William Thomas. (Source: S. Brown.)

On 9 October, William boarded the troopship *HMT Assaye*, and with the rest of his battalion set sail for India, landing at Bombay on 10 November. He was too old for fighting, but he could offer valuable experience at the British garrison, and it is possible, given his later duties in Dorchester, that he was part of the prison guard at the internment camp at Ahmednagar.[209]

On 15 February 1915, William was admitted to hospital at Ahmednagar, complaining of pains in some of his joints. This was diagnosed as rheumatic fever and he was transferred to the station hospital at Ambala and then another at Dagshai. It was at the latter that William was diagnosed with the initial stages of valvular heart disease. As a consequence he was sent back to England in August 1918, but not with a discharge from the Army. Instead he was posted to guard prisoners at Dorchester. For William this cloud had a silver lining, because his family home, at 1 Maie Terrace, literally overlooked the camp. It is not known whether he was allowed to stay with his wife Ellen and his children when not on duty, but he certainly saw more of his family than most of the other guards. William's stint at the camp lasted until 31 March 1916, when he was finally discharged, returning to his civilian employment as a carpenter and joiner. His illness did not seem to affect him unduly, and, like Reuben Isaacson, he presented himself again for service to his country, this time as an air raid warden in Dorchester during WW2. He died in 1944.

This intricately carved wooden box was made by one of the prisoners, who gave it to William Thomas as a gift. (Source: S. Brown.)

Pte George Squibb
1st Btn Dorsetshire Rgt

George Squibb was born in Sutton Poyntz, a village just to the east of the town of Weymouth, in 1879. After the birth of their third child, he and his wife Emily moved to a cottage on The Ridgeway, opposite the Old Ship Inn in Upwey, and there they went on to have four more children. William was a stonemason with the Great Western Railway and in 1915 he volunteered for the 1st Btn Dorsets and became part of the National Reserve, looking after prisoners in Dorchester.

209 A large internment camp had been formed at Ahmednagar, to house most of the adult males in India of foreign nationality.

George Squibb in his Dorset Regiment uniform. This photo was doubtless taken just before he went to France. (Source: R. Hoadley.)

George Squibb, with wife Emily and their children, outside their house, where Emily was admonished by her neighbours for giving water to thirsty prisoners. (Source: R. Hoadley.)

George remained at the camp until he was mobilised and sent to France in March 1917, but before he left he went back to Sutton Poyntz to say goodbye to his mother, who lived in Puddledock Lane. She told him to take care and not to be a hero, because he had seven children waiting for him when he got home. His response to her concern was to say that should he not return, God would care for them. Sadly, George did not return, lasting just 3 weeks of fighting. He died on 16 April 1917 after being wounded at Cepy Farm, near St Quinton, France.[210] The *Upwey Parish Magazine* reported his death, saying, 'He believed very firmly that God would answer the prayers of his wife and family by bringing him safely through. But the answer for them too has been that the cup may not pass away from them unless they drink it, and we ask God that they learn to say with their redeemer "thy will be done" and that His angel from Heaven will strengthen them through their agony.'

210 The personal details were told to me by George's granddaughter.

L/Sgt Robert Clifford Johnson – 101682
6 Coy RAMC

Robert Johnson. (Source: S. Stainer.)

Robert Johnson was a Yorkshire man who lived with his parents, William and Ada, at their home in Brighouse, West Yorkshire. Robert worked as a grocer's assistant and at the age of 19 joined the Army on 6 September 1915. His army record indicates that he was recruited for home service only, suggesting that he was not medically A1. Accordingly, he joined 6 Coy RAMC and spent some time at Queen Alexandra's Military Hospital at Cosham, near Portsmouth, before being transferred to work at the hospital in Dorchester's prison camp.

Robert remained at the camp until 1 January 1920, when he left the Army with a disability pension of 12 shillings per week. The reason for the pension was that a medical board had concluded that he was suffering from heart trouble, attributable to his war service. Although Robert left the Army, he did not leave Dorchester, but settled in the town, living at Elton Villas, Monmouth Road. He died in 1958.

Pte Fred Green

Fred Green was another Dorset man who became a prison guard at the camp, although exactly how he became one and for what period he was there is unknown. The proof of his connection with the camp comes from a photograph in which he appears. His age and the fact that he was a local man suggest that he was part of one of the two National Reserve battalions raised locally, or he joined the RDC.

Fred, who was born in 1867, was employed as a coal porter and lived with his wife Minnie and his eight children at 60 Holloway Road, Dorchester. He gave to his country in more than one way during the course of the War, losing two of his sons, Thomas and Joseph. Thomas Green joined the local regiment in Dorchester and went missing during the 5th Btn's ill-fated attack on trenches at Susak Kuyu, during the Gallipoli campaign, on 21 August

Curious Dorchester folk look on as Fred Green (foreground) and other soldiers of the RDC escort a contingent of military prisoners to their new home in Dorchester's POW camp. (Courtesy of Dorset County Museum.)

1915, although his death was not confirmed until May 1917. Joseph Green, a year younger than his brother, died of disease on 19 October 1919 whilst serving with the Dorsets in India. Fred died in 1925, aged 60.

Appendix 1: The Hague Convention

The Hague Convention of 1907 was the culmination of a number of international conferences that resulted in a series of treaties and conventions on the conduct of war.

The 1907 conference was the last before the outbreak of the Great War. It was signed on 18 October 1907 and came into force on 26 January 1910. The conventions relating to the treatment and responsibilities of prisoners of war are shown below.

- Prisoners of war are in the power of the hostile Government, but not of the individuals or corps who capture them.

  They must be humanely treated.

  All their personal belongings, except arms, horses, and military papers, remain their property.

- Prisoners of war may be interned in a town, fortress, camp, or other place, and bound not to go beyond certain fixed limits; but they cannot be confined except as an indispensable measure of safety and only while the circumstances which necessitate the measure continue to exist.

- The State may utilize the labour of prisoners of war according to their rank and aptitude, officers excepted. The tasks shall not be excessive and shall have no connection with the operations of the war.

  Prisoners may be authorized to work for the public service, for private persons, or on their own account.

  Work done for the State is paid for at the rates in force for work of a similar kind done by soldiers of the national army, or, if there are none in force, at a rate according to the work executed.

  When the work is for other branches of the public service or for private persons the conditions are settled in agreement with the military authorities. The wages of the prisoners shall go towards improving their position, and the balance shall be paid them on their release, after deducting the cost of their maintenance.

- The Government into whose hands prisoners of war have fallen is charged with their maintenance.

  In the absence of a special agreement between the belligerents, prisoners of war shall be treated as regards board, lodging, and on the same footing as the troops of the Government who captured them.

- Prisoners of war shall be subject to the laws, regulations, and orders in force in the army of the State in whose power they are. Any act of insubordination justifies the adoption towards them of such measures of severity as may be considered necessary.

  Escaped prisoners who are retaken before being able to rejoin their own army or before leaving the territory occupied by the army which captured them are liable to disciplinary punishment. Prisoners who, after succeeding in escaping, are again taken prisoners, are not liable to any punishment on account of the previous flight.

- Every prisoner of war is bound to give, if he is questioned on the subject, his true name and rank, and if he infringes this rule, he is liable to have the advantages given to prisoners of his class curtailed.

- Prisoners of war may be set at liberty on parole if the laws of their country allow, and, in such cases, they are bound, on their personal honour, scrupulously to fulfil, both towards their own Government and the Government by whom they were made prisoners, the engagements they have contracted.

  In such cases their own Government is bound neither to require of nor accept from them any service incompatible with the parole given.

- A prisoner of war cannot be compelled to accept his liberty on parole; similarly the hostile Government is not obliged to accede to the request of the prisoner to be set at liberty on parole.

- Prisoners of war liberated on parole and recaptured bearing arms against the Government to whom they had pledged their honour, or against the allies of that Government, forfeit their right to be treated as prisoners of war, and can be brought before the courts.

- Individuals who follow an army without directly belonging to it, such as newspaper correspondents and reporters, sutlers[211] and contractors, who fall into

211 An army camp follower who sold goods to the soldiers.

the enemy's hands and whom the latter thinks expedient to detain, are entitled to be treated as prisoners of war, provided they are in possession of a certificate from the military authorities of the army which they were accompanying.

- An inquiry office for prisoners of war is instituted on the commencement of hostilities in each of the belligerent States, and, when necessary, in neutral countries which have received belligerents in their territory. It is the function of this office to reply to all inquiries about the prisoners. It receives from the various services concerned full information respecting internments and transfers, releases on parole, exchanges, escapes, admissions into hospital, deaths, as well as other information necessary to enable it to make out and keep up to date an individual return for each prisoner of war. The office must state in this return the regimental number, name and surname, age, place of origin, rank, unit, wounds, date and place of capture, internment, wounding, and death, as well as any observations of a special character. The individual return shall be sent to the Government of the other belligerent after the conclusion of peace.

  It is likewise the function of the inquiry office to receive and collect all objects of personal use, valuables, letters, etc., found on the field of battle or left by prisoners who have been released on parole, or exchanged, or who have escaped, or died in hospitals or ambulances, and to forward them to those concerned.

- Relief societies for prisoners of war, which are properly constituted in accordance with the laws of their country and with the object of serving as the channel for charitable effort shall receive from the belligerents, for themselves and their duly accredited agents, every facility for the efficient performance of their humane task within the bounds imposed by military necessities and administrative regulations. Agents of these societies may be admitted to the places of internment for the purpose of distributing relief, as also to the halting places of repatriated prisoners, if furnished with a personal permit by the military authorities, and on giving an undertaking in writing to comply with all measures of order and police which the latter may issue.

- Inquiry offices enjoy the privilege of free postage. Letters, money orders, and valuables, as well as parcels by post, intended for prisoners of war, or dispatched by them, shall be exempt from all postal duties in the countries of origin and destination, as well as in the countries they pass through.

- Presents and relief in kind for prisoners of war shall be admitted free of all import or other duties, as well as of payments for carriage by the State railways.

- Officers taken prisoners shall receive the same rate of pay as officers of corresponding rank in the country where they are detained, the amount to be ultimately refunded by their own Government.

- Prisoners of war shall enjoy complete liberty in the exercise of their religion, including attendance at the services of whatever church they may belong to, on the sole condition that they comply with the measures of order and police issued by the military authorities.

- The wills of prisoners of war are received or drawn up in the same way as for soldiers of the national army. The same rules shall be observed regarding death certificates as well as for the burial of prisoners of war, due regard being paid to their grade and rank.

- After the conclusion of peace, the repatriation of prisoners of war shall be carried out as quickly as possible.

Appendix 2: Known Inspections of the Dorchester Camp

Date	Inspection
11/1914	(Germany)
1/1915	Eduard Naville & Victor Van Bercham (ICRC)
4/2/1915	Robert B. Jackson (USA)
1/12/1915	Mr Lowry (USA)
12/1915	John Van der Veer (Dutch)
1/6/1916	(USA)
31/7/1916	(USA)
20/8/1916	Dr A. Taylor (USA)
29/3/1917	Dr F. Schwyzer (Swiss)
5/10/1917	Maj. J.L. Isler (Swiss)
11/6/1918	Mon. C. Orelli & Dr A. de Sturler (Swiss)
28/3/1919	Drs A. de Sturler & R. de Sturler (Swiss)

Appendix 3: Camps Under the Jurisdiction of Dorchester[212]

Agricultural camps

The Workhouse, Axbridge, Somerset
Beaminster, Dorset
Binegar, Gurney Slade, Somerset
Brailes, Chipping Norton, Oxon
Brightwell, Wallingford, Berks
Chapel Oak, Iron Cross, Salford Priors, Warks
Avon House, Chippenham, Wilts
Evesham, Worcs
Great Hampton House, Evesham, Worcs
Hallatrow, Shepton Mallet, Somerset
Honiton, Devon
Lambourne, attached Compton agricultural depot, Berks
Northleach, Glos
Starcross, Devon
Stoulton, Whittington, Worcs
Stowell, attached Gillingham agricultural depot, Somerset
Swanage, Dorset
Tiverton, attached Dulverton agricultural depot, Devon
Wantage, Berks
Little Canford Farmhouse, Wimborne, Dorset
Winchcombe, Glos, attached Toddington agricultural depot
Drill Hall, Woodstock, Oxon
Wool, Dorset
Wootton Bassett, attached Devizes agricultural depot, Wilts

Agricultural depots

Banbury, Oxon
Kempshott House, Basingstoke, Hants
Blaisdon, Longhope, Glos
Cholsey, Devon
Compton, Berks
Devizes, Wilts
Doverdale, Droitwich, Worcs
Dulverton, Somerset
Eardiston, Tenbury Wells, Worcs
Iwerne Minster, Dorset
Little Woodcote, Kenilworth, Warks

212 List taken from Mark (2007).

The Tannery, Keyford, Somerset
Kingsbridge, Devon
Perham Down, Salisbury, Wilts
Rochford House, Tenbury Wells, Worcs
Shepton Mallet, Somerset
Soho Pool, Hookley, Birmingham, West Midlands
Coronation Hall, South Brent, Devon
Brightwell, Watlington, Oxon

Agricultural depot/work camps
Gillingham, Dorset

Agricultural/work camps
Bradford Abbas, Dorset

Civilian work camps
Bulford, Wilts
Monkspath, Warks
Pershore, Worcs

Work camps
Alton, Hants
Atherstone, Warks
Badsay Manor, Badsay, Worcs
Berkswell, Hampton-in-Arden, Warks
Blandford, Dorset
Bovington, Dorset
The Priory, Broad Marston, Mickleton, Glos
Brockenhurst, Hants
Castle Bromwich, Birmingham, West Midlands
Cheltenham, Glos
Cheriton Bishop, Exeter, Devon
Hillside House, Chipping Norton, Oxon
Chiseldon, Swindon, Wilts
Churchdown, Glos
Churt, Farnham, Surrey
Cirencester, Glos
Codford, Wilts
College Town, Camberley, Surrey
Cove, Farnborough, Hants
Crichel, Blandford, Dorset
Barlecombe House, Dulverton, Somerset
Eggesford House, Eggesford, Devon
Pidnell House, Faringdon, Berks
Craycombe House, Fladbury, Pershore, Worcs
Flowerdown, Winchester, Hants
Fovant, Hants
Frampton-on-Seven, Stonehouse, Glos
Great Whitley, Wilts

Hatherleigh, Devon
Hawkesbury Upton, Glos
Combe Raleigh House, Honiton, Devon
Hursley Park, Winchester, Hants
Ilchester, Somerset
Lee Mill, Ivybridge, Devon
Ladroke Hall, Ladbroke, Warks
Larkhill, Wilts
Lawford Hill, Warks
Leigh, Worcs
Leighterton, Glos
The Workhouse, Long Ashton, Bristol, Somerset
Marcham, Abingdon, Berks
Martley, Worcs
The Aerodrome, Netheravon, Wilts
The Institute, Newton Abbott, Devon
Ashbury Court, North Lew, Devon
Northfield, Worcs
Offchurch Bury, Leamington, Warks
Peopleton, Pershore, Worcs
Radford, Warks
Bamey Farm, Ramsbury, Wilts
Romsey, Hants
Saltram, Devon
Sandhill Park, Somerset
Shelsley Walsh, Worcs
Shirehampton, Bristol, Somerset
Shottery, Stratford-on-Avon, Warks
Sidbury, Sidmouth, Devon
Soberton, Bishops Waltham, Hants
Unicorn Hotel, South Molton, Devon
Stowell, Wincanton, Somerset
Sutton Veny, Warminster, Wilts
Thornbury, Glos
Toddington, Glos
Tutnall and Cobley, Worcs
Twyford, Berks
Upavon, Wilts
Holly Lodge, Wellesborne, Warwick
Weston on the Green, Bicester, Oxon
Wimborne, Dorset
Winchcombe, Glos
Witney, Oxon
Woodstock, Oxon
Wookey, Wells, Somerset
Comer House, Wooton Bassett, Wilts
Worthy Down, Hants
Yatesbury, Calne, Wilts

Sources

Primary sources

Alien Enemies of Military Age – Detention of Prisoners of War. National Archives, HO45/10760/269116.

Borough of Dorchester Burial Records. Dorchester Town Council.

Cannock Chase German Military Cemetery Burial Records.

Detention of Enemy Aliens as Prisoners of War, 1914–1915. National Archives, HO45/10760/269116.

Deutsche Blätter des Kriegsgefangenenlagers Dorchester, 24 December 1916. Bundesarchiv, MSG200/1878.

Documents relating to theatre performances. Bundesarchiv, MA/200/1878 and MSG200/1957.

German Prisoners in Great Britain (1916) – series of photographs taken by the Photographic Unit of the Royal Flying Corps. www.archive.org.

German Prisoners of War: Camp in England for Non-Commissioned Officers and Men. Film made by Royal Flying Corps Photographic Unit (1917). Imperial War Museum.

House of Commons Parliamentary Debates, 11 May and 13 May 1915. (Hansard.)

House of Lords Parliamentary Debates, 23 March 1916. (Hansard.)

Plüschow, Kapitänleutnant Gunther (1922) *My Escape from Donnington Hall, Preceded by an Account of the Siege of Kaio-Chow*. John Lane, London.

Proposed Release of Civilians Interned in the British and German Empires. Government White Paper. HMSO, London.

Reports of visits of inspection to internment camps. National Archives, FO383/276.

Schmidt-Reder, Bruno (1915) *In England Kriegsgefangen! Meine Erlebnisse in dem Gefangenenlager Dorchester*. (Prisoner in England! My Experiences in the Dorchester Prison Camp.) Georg Bath, Berlin.

de Sturler, Dr A. (1919) *Swiss Legation Report of a Visit to Dorchester POW Camp, 7/4/1919*. National Archives, FO383/506.

Taylor, Dr (1916) *Survey on the Diet of Prisoners of War in Dorchester, Sept, 1916*. National Archives, FO383/506.

Treatment of German Prisoners of War and Interned Civilians in the United Kingdom. Correspondence between HM Government and the American Ambassador, March 1915. HMSO, London.

Treatment of Prisoners of War in England and Germany During the First Eight Months of the War (1915). HMSO, London.

Secondary sources

Bates, Brian (2012) *Dorchester Remembers the Great War*. Roving Press.

Hardy, F. E. (1962) *The Life of Thomas Hardy, 1840–1928*. Macmillan Press.

Hearing, M. (2000) *The Book of Martinstown*. Winterborne St Martin Parish Council.

Jackson, Robert (1989) *Behind the Wire. The Prisoners, 1914–1918*. Routledge.

Jones, Heather (2013) *Violence Against Prisoners of War in the First World War: Britain, France and Germany, 1914–1920*. (Studies in the Social and Cultural History of Modern Warfare.) Cambridge University Press.

Machray, Robert (*c*. 1918) *Great Britain's Humane Treatment of German Prisoners of War*. Chapter CCLXXVIL of *The Great War – The Standard History of the World-Wide Conflict*. Historical Section of the Committee of Imperial Defence.

Mark, Graham (2007) *Prisoners of War in British Hands During WWI: a Study of Their History, the Camps and their Mails*. The Postal History Society.

Panayi, Panikos (2012) *Prisoners of Britain. German Civilian and Combatant Internees During the First World War*. Anchester University Press.

Skyrme, J.E. (ed. E. Rowbotham) (1993) *A Casterbridge Ironmonger*. E. Rowbotham.

Yarnall, John (2011) *Barbed Wire Disease. British and German Prisoners of War, 1914–1918*. The History Press.

Newspapers

Aftenposten, Norway
Auckland Star, New Zealand
Border Watch, Mount Gambier, Australia
Charleston Sunday News, USA
Dorset County Chronicle and the Somersetshire Gazette
Dorset Echo
Manchester Evening News
Marlborough Express
Midland Daily Telegraph
Newcastle Daily Journal
New York Times
Reading Eagle, Pennsylvania, USA
Somerset County Herald
Taunton Courier and Advertiser
The Church times
The London Times
Western Gazette
Western Times.
York Post and Leeds Intelligencer

Websites

Ancestry: www.ancestry.co.uk
Europeana 1914–1918: www.europeana1914-1918.eu
Findmypast: www.findmypast.co.uk
International Committee of the Red Cross: www.icrc.org
Internet Archive: www.archive.org
Prisoners of War, 1914–1918: www.prisonersofwar1914-1918

About the Author

Brian Bates has lived in Dorchester with his wife Doreen and two daughters since 1971. His love of social and economic history was ignited by John Haley, an inspirational schoolmaster, and his particular passion for the history of Dorchester began when he wrote a thesis on the town's 17th-century economy. For him, 'real history' is the story of the ordinary person and their communities, especially when they find themselves in extraordinary predicaments. Brian gives talks on aspects of the town's history, particularly during the 17th century and the Victorian and Edwardian periods. Previous publications include *Dorchester Remembers the Great War* (published by Roving Press, www.rovingpress.co.uk), a tribute to those who are listed on Dorchester's Great War memorials, a transcription of the diary of William Whiteway, a 17th-century Dorchester merchant, and three military biographies.

Index